S

C000079731

fragments
pieces of autobiography

'Margaret Buckley died in 1992, before she could
see the respect her tight, taut fictions achieved.'
Nicholas Lezard, *The Guardian*

Margaret Buckley's life was crammed with inner
excitement, inward achievement, both personal and
literary. The literary was derived from the personal,
which makes these autobiographical sketches of
special interest to admirers of her novels. They have
the same intrinsic qualities of vivid and honest first-
hand responsiveness. Assembled from poems,
essays, draft novels and diaries, fragmentary and
fortuitous, they provide a mosaic of impressions of
a sensibility developing from inexperienced girl to
mature novelist. For the most part written
immediately after the events they describe, they
give the feel of her experience undisguised by the
long-term memory that bedevils autobiography.

The names of living people have been generally
altered. If they are nonetheless recognized, it must
be remembered that the portraits here are not so
much descriptions of the people as projections of
the author's imagination, and are included here as
representative of that alone.

MARGARET BUCKLEY

Born in London in 1930, Margaret Buckley was the child of a clerk in the London Docks. After a degree in English at London University and some years school-teaching she moved with her husband to Cornwall where her daughter was born. In 1961 they made a final move to Kenilworth in Warwickshire, where she began writing novels and literary criticism. In 1980 she was diagnosed with breast cancer. The remission of the disease began to give way almost as soon as *The Commune* was completed. She died in 1992.

MARGARET BUCKLEY

fragments

pieces of autobiography

THE CHRYSALIS PRESS

First published 2006
by the Chrysalis Press
7 Lower Ladyes Hills, Kenilworth CV8, England
email: sales@margaretbuckley.com
www.margaretbuckley.com

ISBN: 1897765 10X

Printed in Great Britain

For Jane and Hannie

Contents

fragments

PIECES OF AUTOBIOGRAPHY

Child and Student

I had slept, but it was hot and my sleep had been superficial and restless. There was very little space between the top of the Morrison shelter and my head so I did not attempt to sit up. There had probably been many flying bombs during the night but I hadn't heard them and didn't worry about them. I merely wanted to sleep again.

In the distance I heard the very soft and intermittent drone of a doodle-bug. I noticed a rusty flake of metal hanging from the top of the shelter and brushed it off; it fell on my bed. The drone was getting louder very quickly now, it seemed a part of the heat and restlessness; it did not matter, I had heard plenty of them before. I thought I was learning to experience fear philosophically. When I was taking gas at the dentist's I had succeeded, until I saw the leaves outside the window quiver and become a haze.

There was a large pattern on the floor. I imagined it was a vast common and I but a speck on it, far away from flying bombs.

I listened intently to the noise of the engine, it was rather loud and its throb was very regular. I wished the top of the shelter was not black, it is such a sordid, hopeless colour. It would not be long now till it stopped. As it came nearer it rattled, the vibration seemed to shake the house. The rattling and chugging became exceedingly loud, it seemed to be just over the roof. The noise couldn't possibly grow louder, it was surely at its utmost pitch. I hated the noise, but it must not stop.

I turned over to lie on my stomach with my hands over my ears, and stared blankly at the caging that enclosed me. I had to suppress the scream that was surging up within me. My face was slightly damp with a cold sweat. The noise ceased abruptly. There was complete silence, a fearful silence that seemed to drag the air out of the room. Everything was waiting, waiting.

It would not kill me, I had too much to do in my life. This would be just another experience, it would not be the end of all music, all reading, of friendship, love.

There was a thud and a devastating, rending crack. Soot came down in a cloud from the chimney. I coughed. There was a black suspension in the air.

Spring 1947

> You must love as you must eat,
> It's part of nature's plan.
> If a man you love a woman,
> If you're not you love a man.
> Life makes no individuals
> For in everyone that lives
> There's a longing for experience
> That takes but nothing gives.
> Your life and mind and actions
> Can depend upon another

But who wants to have an entity
If one can have a lover?

Summer 1947

I have lain warm-cloistered in a form
Pressed into wood and flattened in a wall,
Have been the dust, as if its consciousness,
And thought myself out of dimension.
But suddenly to know that I am tall,
And feel the hard ground's rigidness
Beat up through me into the sky,
To know my legs must part the air
Like fingers drawn through hair!
Are then the fish and tree in me?
I feel and know all objects and all motion.
I am real and am creation.

1950

Lectures at Bedford College are regarded as compulsory and I attend regularly. This is what schooling means to me: sitting in a classroom and dreaming. I take notes but hardly ever look at them again. They are a way of disposing of the garbage – in at the ear and out at the pen. At school too the teachers were all the time throwing ideas and formulas at me, but they didn't take hold unless I really needed them – I've got some sort of anti-stick on me. Sometimes I let my pen rest to stare out of the window at the gardens. Once the professor – the most boring of them all – paused in her lecture long enough for me to realise she was waiting for me to pick up my pen to continue writing.

My tutor, E.G. Midgeley, has only just completed his research degree at Oxford. He is fair and slight with a rather vague, academic sex interest that suits his role. His appreciation of the presence of a woman takes the form of an over-gallant dalliance. He helps me off with my coat, hangs it up, attempts a searching, sensual look – at least, I feel that's what he's attempting – but succeeds only in something rather like the look he has when he is beginning to get going in an argument. I don't dislike him, I find him sexually negative and unstimulating as a person, but as my tutor, impressing me with his infinite resources of scholarship – this is extremely stimulating. I relish every minute of it.

My essays are usually provocative; partly because of my youth, partly because I express myself passionately. He enjoys them – he feels he can enjoy the woman through her essays, the fumes of the relationship affect his outlook on life – it turns him into a delicate, quivering, vibrant instrument. He remains rooted in himself, keeps himself intact, but is played upon deliciously by the experience of talking, seeing, even touching.

Quite apart from this delightful state of mental intoxication that he and I have evolved between us, a rarefied private atmosphere that doesn't seem to affect the other two women who are generally at the tutorial, his tutorials give me the sense of having an infinitely precious inner and mental life, a life that could go on ceaselessly developing through book and discussion – encompass my whole being, the whole world of understanding, without my taking part in life as a dramatic entity; and he is the custodian of this mental life, he dedicates himself to it, he denies himself for it. He successfully gives the impression of crucifying the flesh for it, but to me it seems when I am outside the tutorials that the battle within him can't be a fierce one. His poor little body is chirpy-in-despair, which takes the measure of the struggle.

February 1951
One day recently while I was drinking coffee after lunch, the two girls who share tutorials with me came up with theirs and sat on either side.

'Old Midge gets worse,' said a tall girl with a rather splayed nose and jet-black short straight hair. 'He's such a damned old bore droning on and on about *Comus* – labouring it like mad when everyone knows it's no cop and no credit to him for labouring the point. I don't know why you stick up for the silly thing, it only makes him go on longer.'

I was instantly angry: 'He dislikes it for the wrong reasons –'

'Oh God, don't let's start one of your expositions now, I only wanted to put it to you, if I could, not to let him get you going, it's all he wants you know, just to have someone madly interested in what he's saying, good or bad, and on the strength of it he goes bumbling on, saying the same things for the whole bloody tutorial.'

I sympathised with this aspect of affairs but there were certain things I just couldn't let go. I didn't say anything but sipped my coffee and offered a cigarette to the excruciating fair-haired bore on my right. Jocelyn took one and fiddled fussily in her handbag for a light so I pushed over my lighter. 'What do you think, Jocelyn – does it all bore you beyond measure, do you wish I'd keep my mouth shut?'

'No, really, I rather like to hear you two going it, however long – I think it's interesting – I wonder where you get your strange ideas from.'

'Good – then for your sake I dare say we'll continue.' I knew why Jocelyn liked it. She was an assiduous brain-picker. 'Did you do anything nice over the weekend,' I asked – 'go out with Robert?'

'Mmm. We went for a wonderful walk in St James's Park and then to see *Carmen Jones*, it was terrific. Sunday we went to tea with Robert's parents. They're awfully nice, they treat me as if they really want to see us marry, not like some prospective parents-in-law looking for ways of prising their son's hooks off you. Robert is getting a little hard to handle now though. His parents left us alone for a while and we were talking about *Carmen Jones* and so on and he kept fiddling with the strap of my dress. I was wearing that green cocktail dress of mine, you know, the one I wore at the end-of-term party. Well, I took no notice – but suddenly I felt the strap flop on to my arm. I pushed it up again and he pushed it down again and kissed my neck and shoulders so passionately I didn't know what to do – I tried to make him sit up again but he kept leaning over me more and his other hand started moving around my neck and down the front of my dress. I stopped him of course and he apologised but you could see he didn't mean it; the apology I mean. Honestly if we don't get married soon I don't know what I'm going to do about him.'

I always feel as if I can't breathe after listening to Jocelyn for a time. She looks and sounds so dull, so half-alive that it's as if the air has suddenly become thick and sleepy and unrefreshing and I want to breathe deeply and leap out of the chair, if only to prove that I can still move quickly and strongly and to get back the normal rhythm of my life. Her thick turned-up nose was directed towards my lighter on the table, she was half thinking about the episode, half waiting for my response, and was slowly banishing the blush she had raised at this little confession while flicking at the corner of a women's magazine with her engagement finger. I sometimes catch her meditating on that ring in tutorials and lectures – philosophising about it, absorbed with its merits. I don't know how anyone as boring as Jocelyn ever makes a man interested in her enough to do more than pass the salt or talk about the weather, and there she is engaged.

May 1951

I like to work in the gardens of the Holme, overlooking the lake. It is used exclusively by the English department. Sometimes I look back at it and feel an acute longing – a pang of pleasure at the adventure in thought and feeling and argument that the place represents in my imagination. My whole body seems to be yearning for it. I have a longing to be filled with the experience of reading, reading books that you don't imagine could have any contact with you until suddenly they leap to life for you like a birth and you become filled with ideas and new experience and carry them with you for days.

Donne's poetry, for instance, laying open the underlying conflicts he finds in living, crushing out the last drop of intellectual – or in the long run spiritual – satisfaction from his experiences, in an effort to understand each one and fit them all in. He interprets and analyses his reactions and experiences according to what he finds as an individual. The significance of the universe is focused in the effects it produces on him – using himself as a prism: things split into their different colours according to his facets.

August 1951

Waitressing in Uncle Harry's café in Leyton. It is very small – the serving counter stretches almost from wall to wall – just long enough to have two people abreast to be served. The pale yellow plastic tops of the tables and the rather less sick cream of the walls depress me excessively. But there's an attraction I can't resist, in the shape of my cousin Cliff.

At the end of the counter is a door in a partition, the only place one can stand, when in the bar, and not be observed by the people in the café. I sometimes push open this door and feel something thick and soft behind it. I squeeze through, to be grabbed fiercely and pulled tight up against a large male body. My bowels lurch with excitement whenever he pounces on me and kisses me, I tingle and then became molten as his mouth buries into mine. Cliff always kisses me at great length and after a while the flood of desire that he arouses in me ebbs away and I'm left to myself, thinking, Honestly, how can he go on like this, what does he think I am? – he can't be feeling anything all this time – he's gone mad over a mouth. But he shifts his hold on me, grabs my body afresh and feels it with large searching hands that hurt, and my desire comes back obliterating me.

Once as I was coming to the surface of consciousness again I heard a chuckle behind me. I came out in a faint sweat of panic and embarrassment and broke from his arms to go over to the counter. The old woman was probably thinking aloud – at all events she hadn't seen us, she was staring at the slowly steaming windows, completely cut off from her surroundings. I couldn't look at Cliff, I knew he would look raw and his eyes be narrowed and as sharp as a hunting cat's, with an incongruous soft look of suffering behind it. I knew this would soon give place to a rather stupid dazed look and an over-relaxed mouth. I felt him moving up behind me to the counter and my hand trembled as I started to butter some rolls with the greasy knife left from the previous night....

Otherwise, the tedious tasks of the café, serving, clearing tables, emptying ashtrays, smiling and commenting, take up a lot of energy and leave me feeling empty, tired and yet restless. The one factor in this routine that raises my spleen, brings me out of my apathetic automatism to a point where I give up, go through the serving area into the back yard and smoke is the sickening habit of tipping and all its accompanying degradations. Generally a tip is left on the table unostentatiously and in clearing I pick it up and put it in the till when I take the crockery out. Cliff notices this with amusement and never mentions it. Sometimes however a particularly loud and vulgar man – it is always a man – insists on my taking a tip personally. He closes my hand round it and winks with an absurd look composed of a leer and paternal understanding, as if this fourpence were my price and he was paying it. Or a coin is slipped into the pocket of my apron and smiles and looks of self-congratulation offered until he leaves the café. I am eaten up with shame over such trifles. I usually manage to smile and leave quickly to put the coin in the till. It poisons my hand until I've put it in the dustbin-till.

October 1951
Being with Cliff has alerted me to other men. I am to be a bridesmaid at his wedding and I'm having my dress made up by the wife of his best friend, who shows an interest in me. I reciprocate. One evening at their house I went upstairs to the loo and going into the bathroom to wash and put fresh powder on I remembered I'd left my handbag on the floor of the lavatory. As I went out to get it I heard a man's footsteps coming down the passage so I instinctively stepped back into the bathroom. I waited there full of suspense and excitement to see what would happen. After a few moments he said something to me through the half-open door that I couldn't understand.

I pulled the door open further and said, 'Pardon?' I saw him standing there with my handbag in his hand looking extremely tense and quite unable to say what he wanted to say. I took the bag and said thank you and moved as if to go out and get past him. Instantly our arms went round each other and he kissed me. When the kiss was over we stood holding each other, I was resting my face against his breast. We didn't look into each other's faces and yet we were relieved that at last we'd admitted to each other. The suspense at least was over. I was holding my bag hard into the small of his back and this at last made him realise where we were. He didn't attempt to look at me but kissed my hair and the side of my head softly and brought up his hand and slid it under my hair and around my neck. He caressed my neck with his fingers and then tightened his grasp around it and pulled my head back and kissed me again more tenderly. I was completely passive, given up to delight. I waited in his arms without thought or notion of what I must do next, waiting for his decisions. An abrupt movement in the room on the other side of the passage made us spring apart suddenly. I was filled with a scalding sensation, a mixture of embarrassment, guilt and a sense of nakedness and bereavement. He stood there quite still for a moment trying to collect his thoughts, suffering a flood of awareness. In a short time he had come to an understanding of the situation, he left me instantly and went back into the lounge.

Now I was left alone in the bathroom I mechanically went to the hand basin, shivering. I washed and powdered my face, which looked bright but pale. As I saw myself I was filled with a sense of futility and insufficiency: No, not this all over again – it's so miserable. I tried to make myself think in the conventional terms of love. Did I want to marry him? The question didn't seem to mean a thing. It was like saying to a bather, 'Do you intend to train for the Olympics?'

Two days later I was sitting in their lounge with him while his wife and my mother discussed the dress alterations in the fitting area behind a curtain in the same room. I accepted a cup of coffee from the wide, thick-wristed hand that was stretched in front of me. I heard a thump and with horror and joy saw that he was on his knees. I became rigid as I felt the black wavy head bury its face into my lap. The head and neck were overpowering, I couldn't move – the warmth of his face penetrated slowly through my thighs. The curtain rings clattered aside and his wife came through. In an instant he was looking on the floor for something. When I understood what was happening I wanted to laugh so badly that I had to bite the inside of my lip until it hurt.

February 1952

I've grown sick now with the futility of my relationship with Midgeley – of trying to find *him* in order to challenge him. In despair of this I still charge the old windmills he sticks up in front of me; and leave the tutorials with the glamour of the relationship quickly effervescing and the emptiness and pointlessness of the whole procedure establishing itself fast. The wonder of the place has disappeared. I look at the other students and think, yes, they fit, they seem to be getting what they want – but they don't want much! I am full of ideas and responses to the things I read, and although this frequently amuses and interests my tutors, it's not enough – I want a passionate interchange of ideas. I want to challenge these mature adults, question their responses, and argue until I'm exhausted or really convinced. But there is always the barrier of the specific job to be done. This poet one week, another the next. *You didn't find out enough about his other works, did you? Yes, this is a very fine exposition of your ideas but wrongheaded, I feel.* I've grown used to that kind of remark, verbal or written at the foot of my essays. There isn't any point. Many of the lecturers are so confined within a small field of scholastic interest that any life-interest in them was pushed overboard years ago. Those that aren't like this are either too limited in their understanding to be bothered with or too mature to be bothered with me.

May 1952

I have been going for lessons in ballroom dancing, where I've met a man ten years older than myself, married but separated from his wife, a sergeant in the Guards. He has begun taking me to places like nightclubs, which I wouldn't attempt on my own, even if I could afford them, and is simply grateful for a kiss and cuddle in the taxi home.

Going out one evening with him, I walked quickly up the street, feeling with pleasure the pavement beating into the soles of my feet, and enjoyed the jerky rhythm of my high heels jarring the backs of my legs and the noise of the heels echoing loudly. It filled me with a wonderful sense of excitement and anticipation. One or two lights were on in shop windows, I walked towards them as if they were small worlds of warmth and pleasure drawing me to them.

Having reached the main road and its shops, I found their stupid display and dead advertisement pictures tiring. They made my spirit feel exhausted. I hated the crude red trolley buses as they lurched up to the bus stop with their poles crackling, and felt more and more depressed as I watched the tired faces of the men and women getting off and the bus rolling off again with a feeling of destroying apathy. I became depressed and heavy.

As I turned the corner I saw his huge shape covered with an extremely correct light raincoat – from this distance he looked smart, even elegant. My heart was already beating faster and I was beginning to change, to feel light, to glow. He walked quickly towards me and gave me a light, delicate kiss, almost without contact, turned me and made me take his arm. I began to get extremely excited as the evening got darker and the lights came on, I felt almost sick with excitement. The air was moist and exhilarating, we walked perfectly in time. I took a quick glance at his face, which had changed – he looked keen and intelligent, with power in the sensual features – he seemed transformed – I looked away quickly. The lighted bus went by full of purpose and life – it was bright with joy. In a few moments we were running and had boarded a bus that was just beginning to move. The excitement of this made us both laugh and we sat close to each other and smiled into each other's faces while he turned towards me with his hand in his pocket taking out the money. We sat holding hands, intensely absorbed by the lighted shop windows, by the appearance of the passengers who looked as if they were going somewhere new, exciting, full of interest. Their shoulders were vigorous, their smiles confident and intimate; everyone seemed to be in this strange state of exhilaration.

After what seemed a short time we got off the bus and made our way to an underground station. We said nothing or if anything just light-hearted observations on people. I came out of my enchantment sufficiently to ask where we were going. Reg said he had booked some expensive seats for the Old Vic. I was pleased to go but not with him. I felt disappointed in him. What was the good of his trying to win me on my own ground – far better for him to have cut out an evening for us in his own style, something he would have enjoyed. I felt disillusioned and a little flat. What a wretched business it would be. I wouldn't be able to enjoy it because he would be watching me, trying to relish the performance at second hand, trying to feel he fitted. What a fool he was. I despised him for it. He noticed that the temperature was cooler and that some of the radiance had left the earth. He looked quickly and anxiously at me as we turned into the station.

The journey into the centre of London was uncomfortable, awkward. We were aware of people in a different way, I noticed how painfully tense most people were when trying to give the impression of sitting relaxedly and at ease. How embarrassed when they noticed you looking at them; their aggressive assertion of their right to be at ease in front of you, the deliberate swinging of one leg across the other and the reshuffling of the newspaper. They fidgeted me. I wanted to go up to them and say, What's the matter with you! – or tear their damned silly papers out of their hands – oh, they were a deadly, sickening crowd.

Reg tentatively put a hand on my knee. 'You're going to like it this evening, aren't you?'

I felt sorry and compassionate, full of responsibility for liking him enough to lead him on. I took his long-fingered wide hand and slowly threaded each of his fingers between my own and held them there. 'Yes, you know I am,' I answered, smiling at him gently and then looking away.

When we reached Waterloo we found we had nearly three quarters of an hour to spare before the play began. I asked him at last what we were going to see. It was *A Winter's Tale*. I was glad of that, I'd never seen it performed before.

'Shall we have some coffee as we've got so long to wait?' he asked.

I thought that was a good idea. We walked away from the station until we came to a smallish, brilliantly lit, cheerful little café. I sat down at a little red-topped table in a corner bench seat. He brought back two coffees in transparent plastic cups and some plain biscuits. I was glad to see the biscuits – I was hungry. We ate and drank in silence for a while and as we neared the end of the coffee Reg lit a cigarette for me and passed it over.

I sat drawing patterns with my finger in some spilt coffee. I was beginning to feel acutely embarrassed. I'd somehow gone so far away from him that I wondered what on earth I was doing there next to this married stranger. The situation seemed a little horrible and frightening, also a little amusing. I began to smile and laugh in a small, nervous, private fashion. When I dared to look up at him and saw his eyes full of a ridiculous melodramatic appeal mixed with something like surprise I nearly screamed with laughter. I made a kind of high-pitched squeak at the back of my throat that I swallowed instantly and looked seriously at him, blushing and feeling hysterical.

August 1952

Back at the café, with Cliff now living with his wife Doreen and baby in the flat above. It's torture being cooped up again in this tiny little hole of a serving hatch with a man like him. His wife is always opening the door from the side stairs suddenly – blasting it open without having made a sound approaching it. Whenever she does this I feel as if someone has shot me in the stomach and the sharp nasty little burning pain remains there several seconds with my heart fluttering about like a landed fish.

But his wife seldom comes into the café in the early morning so I feel exposed to him while the street outside is thinly populated and the café only a quarter full.

One morning he moved over to me and put down a huge oblong anaemic wodge for me to slice as thin as I dare without personal risk.

'Marge, how about seeing me tonight, please Marge, please – no-one'll know.'

I despised the note of whining that thins his voice whenever he begs me for favours, but at the same time it thrilled me. When I'm attracted to a man I can hardly ever tell anything else about him. I never remember Cliff's saying anything that stimulated or made my intelligent self leap to meet him. I can't recall any depth of experience in his face – any purpose – any real control over himself. His hair oil pronounces him vulgar enough – though it moves me sexually whenever I smell it faintly against a cloth or reeking in his comb.

He was singing behind me, doing some tidying up around the huge stone sink at the back. His voice was very light – youthful – I could tell he was smiling while he was singing:

> 'I wish I were an apple on a tree,
> I wish I were an apple on a tree,
> If I were an apple on a tree
> A girl'd come and take a bite of me…'

– it dwindled to a hum.

He came behind me and leaned towards me. I turned round to look at him. He was smiling one of his peculiarly radiant white-teeth smiles that transform his whole face into something almost delicate, and because of the full mouth and thick nose it was powerfully attractive. His eyes were bright and irresponsible. That was the way to be! I moved over to the partition door feeling the exquisite weight creep from my bowels to my thighs to my knees. He met me with a searing impact. I can never put my arms right round him, he's too wide, and I have to tip my head far back to meet his mouth. I just cling on to his coat, helplessly gripping it for strength to stay upright and not become quite unconscious and dissolved in his kiss. The kiss is a struggle and endurance in itself. He takes all he can in a kiss – it exhausts us both and we feel haunted with dissatisfaction afterwards but while it lasts it burns both of us white. We break away trembling and uncertain of our footing, as if we are walking for the first time after a sickness. The ground seems strangely hard and jarring to walk upon.

I wonder sometimes jealously if he ever kisses Doreen like that. What does it matter if he does, he's nothing to my real self. No, he couldn't, or Doreen wouldn't have that look or that faint nasal ring of complaint in her voice. Then I feel sorry for her: I am being spiteful towards her without intending it and without caring – but if it weren't me it would be someone else that Cliff wanted, it would certainly never be Doreen. I can imagine her tight little embraces offered to him not quite curatively, with the underlying passion to own her wayward husband. Whenever I am left alone with her I feel a calm elation – strong in the sense of my superior femininity.

One evening he was more insistent. I tried to push him off but it was impossible, he'd gripped me hard, his thigh forced hard between my legs, he'd gathered me away from the wall and was pushing my head back until my neck felt pain. I turned my head fiercely away from his and grunted at him and called to him inarticulately to stop – he was groping under my sweater, not as before with a deep, inevitable blind longing but fiercely and painfully. I felt giddy and faint, felt I must give myself up to him, but then sick with panic I squirmed and beat him wildly until he let go and stood in front of me, unbelievably dazed, weak, exposed, and I started to cry with sorrow and relief. He took no notice until I sat and tremblingly tried to find my cigarettes in my handbag. He gave one quick glance of shame, reproof and self-pity. Then he was extremely shy of me and I felt completely alone, as if the world were nothing but dim light and isolation.

'If I disgust you by trying to seduce you all the time, I promise to be well-behaved from now on, a model employer.'

He did disgust me for the moment for having suggested it. Why should a man's desire disgust me, the fool. 'No, you know I find you attractive, that's the main reason why I came back, it's just that I can't stand the strain, and in any case I honestly do feel sorry for Doreen.'

September 1952
At home there is a great deal of mother and daughter affability, no real resentments, no real collisions of will; this is partly because I am the undisputed boss, it makes for peace, even though neither of us really want or enjoy the roles we've somehow cast for ourselves. It is easier for Mum because from childhood I've had that charm in demanding – exacting my own way by smiles – that has now become one of the most effective traits of my personality at home. But I essentially hate bossing – it has somehow been forced upon me by my education, by the silly way my parents assume that because I am clever I must also have a highly forceful, self-sufficient personality.

The warm browns of the livingroom are comforting to me. In the really hot weather the room becomes oppressive but at any other time it gathers the odd furniture into a colour harmony – and it imposes a warm harmony on the superficial relationships of the three who live in it.

Yesterday at teatime I heard Dad's key in the door with the usual queer response of pleasure and recoil.

'Hello darling!' He kissed me on the brow. 'Hello Ma!' he shouted to the kitchen. 'Had a good day?'

Mum came in and turned her cheek for her peck. 'Have you been busy today, dear?' she said. They always ask each other about their days and never listen to the answer. Often the answer isn't given.

'Well, old dear, do you still enjoy café life or have you had enough?' My father treats everything I do, apart from the serious stuff of life, *studying,* as being a whim of mine – growing pains, things I'll grow out of – he understands in his wisdom – it infuriates me.

When I told him I thought of giving up the job, 'Well,' he said, 'you know we don't want the money dear, it was just part of your experience – something you thought would be broadening to do, that's why I never discourage you from anything, it's all experience.'

I winced. It is nearly always the same, he seems to cut life from under my feet, but he's so sane and cares for me so much. I am only just growing out of my father-worship. In my teens it was intermixed with violent rages of hate and rebellion. That chained up my teens; I feel now though, more and more strongly, that liberty is possible and near.

After a few moments of warming his seat in front of a fire that wasn't there he sat down and started to read the newspaper. Soon tea was complete. We were called to take notice and in no hurry took our places.

I usually enjoy my food but am seldom permitted a peaceful enjoyment of it. My father's eyes are upon me for the duration of the meal. He has a nervous way of cramming food into his mouth while talking to me – almost as if the fact that he has food in front of him, the fact that he is forced to eat to keep alive, disgusts him. He does his best to ignore himself eating, he concentrates on me.

He talked and talked, nervously cramming in bread, looking at me. I deliberately took an age to reply.

'Eh, Marg – what do you think, eh?'

I answered as near as possible to not answering.

Mum jumped up and sawed bread violently in front of my nose. The freckled arm passed backwards and forwards in front of my nose, pathetic, nervous – jig, jig.

'You haven't eaten much, Margie dear, why don't you want any more – have you been eating those café cakes?' I was seven years old again.

'No, I haven't, I'm just not hungry.'

My parents suffer my unaccountable nastiness very philosophically – as Dad puts it, 'It's all part of the process of growing away' – and once it's put into words by him, Mum has to accept it, even if she resents it and refuses to understand it – once it is formulated in words she takes it all calmly, seals off her responses, takes it lying down. So I never have the pleasure of seeing them fight back, the process of 'growing away' has to be all one-sided and it is hateful. I make up for it: because they don't fight back I fight them harder to justify myself.

After tea a short walk to Larkswood. Among the trees I came to a small clearing, took off my raincoat and put it neatly on the ground and sat down, breathed deeply and happily, feeling free and unobserved. I leaned backwards on my hands and looked about me, empty of thought or feeling for the moment. The trees were mainly birch with their tall and slender trunks well spaced around me. They had the most exquisite thin grey bark; and the air and the ground around them was moist. I wasn't interested in the leaves, they were beginning to look autumnal – but the trunks were magnificent and the ground so thick with moss and old leaves I'd have liked to thrust my face into them but I was afraid to do it, to get dirty – to have the rotten leaves and the insects on my face and hair. To the left of the clearing was an especially beautiful trunk. I got up and went over to it and fingered it gently and put my hands round it, and the smell of the wood, the moist, living sappiness and the feeling of it so hard and slender under my hands and the smooth-rough surface on my cheek made tears come into my eyes. I was filled with a yearning loneliness, I felt a keen, elated sorrow, my hands looked so long and white and passionate on the tree, so much more beautiful and alive but so separate and dismembered – not belonging anywhere, to any element – incomplete. I was bitterly sorry for my hands. I felt I must share my real experience, I must have a place and belong – I sometimes felt like smoke, being blown about in a light breeze, aimless and indefinite. I gripped the trunk hard until my knuckles turned white, and when I relaxed I had exhausted my yearning – so that eventually I felt refreshed and made keen again, the hard little point of pain giving me a centre.

March 1953

A bout of study induced by panic about Finals. I feel re-infused with life and an intense, clear and simple understanding of it – all the complexities of it absorbed through the medium of literature. I feel completely whole. My eyes stiff with reading and finding it difficult to focus clearly when lifted from the book, I am confronted with a yellow haze outside the library window and blinking turn this haze into a slope of daffodils with trees and blue sky beyond. I want nothing more than to feel warmly enclosed and hushed in the library with the dazzling Spring outside.

Then comes the reaction. Isn't there something slightly obscene, nauseating about what I am doing, churning out ideas, churning out enthusiasm, whipping myself into fettle for sharp, incisive, trenchant criticism – all the little scenes and unreal, worked-up passions for the subject of literature. It's true that I get my deepest – no, not my deepest but my most abiding, all-embracing satisfaction from reading. And some of these books demand an articulate response from me, I have to say what I think and feel about them – but these are rare. To have to write something every fortnight – and to have to try to get to know a piece of work in so short a time if it was good – or to have to force up an interest in that time if it was bad, leaves me with a feeling of sickness and futility. Anyhow what do I care about it? My real life is elsewhere.

I long to get away and start living properly – only I fear that idea is a bigger illusion than the dreams of my university life. I feel deadly cold at such a thought and refuse to give it room for any length of time. Instead I surround it with pleasanter conjectures, those of sharing a life in perfect intimacy with another person and having children – new lives, new problems, new adjustments and a real reason for being alive – these can't be disappointing, this is life itself and I long for it. I want to set my teeth in the meat of life right away – not wait any longer – I feel ready – I even feel my readiness souring, almost as if at 22 I am becoming middle-aged. I feel almost that if I don't become engaged in the business of living soon it will be too late. Perhaps whenever I do face a man, seriously ready to consider him as my life's partner, I'll feel that it is impossible, even ludicrous, and that I don't like him – even worse, that to share my life with him would be a degradation. But perhaps all men are strangers until you marry them. The thought of freezing to death alone or floundering in a viscous mess of unsatisfactory friendships with women tortures me even more – no, any chaos in marriage rather than that. I must fight my way through like everyone else.

Wife and Mother

August 1953

Honeymoon in Cornwall. At the outset of our journey I was glowing with power and brimming with loving impudence. I breathed in deeply and choked on the happiness and excitement lodged in my throat. I slid my hand under Brian's jacket to feel his back through the smooth moving surface of his shirt. The contact stung my hand and I leant against him heavily, deeply happy.

On the train we were forced to get up and move about along the corridors, as best we could over cases and round bodies – to cure the insufferable aches of our backs and legs that had resulted from the fixity of our positions. Our meals were miserable. We were both extraordinarily hungry and I was almost tearfully dissatisfied with the amount I was given to eat and the harassed indifference with which I was served, and felt the screaming frustration of greedily trying to get a spoonful of soup into my mouth without shooting it sideways over the tablecloth and without revealing my indecorous hunger to Brian. Fortunately we fell asleep during the afternoon.

Arriving at Newquay station in the early evening, the impact of the sea air revived me. For a moment I had a brief memory of the morning's excitement and then lapsed back into cold exhaustion as I saw the crowds of people in the streets. I felt the violence in the enormous hotels – the cafés and gift shops battering at their victims on the pavements. Thank God we weren't going to stay in Newquay. I caught a glimpse of the sea – ah, it was marvellous – how beautiful and enormous! – how far it stretched. I saw that it in turn obliterated the buildings – made them nothing. We were standing on the top of a cliff looking down, the whole town was along the cliff top – the waves below us were big and foam-topped; this was the real sea, I couldn't remember having seen sea like this before. I looked over to the harbour – this too was beautiful with its moored boats and long protective arm of wall jutting into the sea. The wind blowing from the sea was incredibly refreshing, I put my head forward and shut my eyes and felt myself coming alive – felt my blood beginning to flow again. I looked at Brian who was moved by the scene and the air, like me, but not quite given up to it. His eyes were dully bright and I felt the restless persistence of his will to get to our room. He bent to my cheek and kissed it.

'Let's catch our bus, we don't know how long it will take us to get to St Mawgan from here or how often the buses run.' He drew me away and back along a path, which led behind the hotels to the bus station.

As I walked I grew more and more fearful of his quickened pace and bright, preoccupied eyes. I hadn't thought about the night ahead of us. When I'd tried to, I'd felt so excited that a real attempt to imagine what it would be like had been impossible. Now this excitement had an edge of fear. I wouldn't look at him. It would seem to be a simple matter, to stop him, put my arms around him, and gain reassurance and comfort that way; but I couldn't do it. He moved swiftly, and with untroubled intent, and there seemed to be no room for it. I walked fast by his side. The wind that beat on one side of us occasionally caught me off balance and pushed me into the shallow ditch that ran alongside the path. I found myself struggling against a rising hysteria. The world was becoming a cold and darkened place, where there was only the unnatural luminosity of fear to guide my thoughts. Blind, black peals of terror ran through me – I was like night, cold, black, empty, dead, with the terror ringing through me, he was a stranger, what on earth was I doing leaning against a strange, over-hot, glistening man – a strange acrid almost odourless perfume was about him.

He was separate and purposeful, abstracted, complete, physically and mentally like a brilliant automaton. I pictured myself running panic-stricken, banging into the crowds, back to the station. My picture of this was brilliantly clear and satisfying. But my body had not moved from his, and the warmth and weight of his hands were a bolt upon me. I was directed by him, his hand on my elbow as my arm held my coat, I was walking without seeing, trying to collect all those normal responses to life that I supposed made up my personality – they weren't there, I was an empty carcase.

I allowed myself to be led to the buses and up the steps of a single-decker that had its engine purring – menacingly, ready to go. That couldn't be our bus – we'd have to wait for ours. I heard Brian whispering that we were lucky – 'Just in time, it'll be an hour and a quarter before the next one.' The thought of waiting an hour and a quarter was extremely attractive to me. I thought desperately of rushing off to the Ladies for five minutes – just long enough to miss the bus – but I was already on and sitting by a window with Brian standing at my side putting the cases in the luggage rack. I wanted to go to sleep. When he sat down I slipped my hand through his arm and put my head on his shoulder and in a few minutes was asleep.

On arrival at St Mawgan, when my eyes became accustomed to being awake I saw that the village was extremely beautiful with a stream running through the centre that was overhung by very tall trees – and with a handsome church on rising ground about 100 yards from the road. The road ran alongside the stream. Just by us and below us in the stream were a couple of local boys intensely preoccupied with selecting stones from the stream from which their bare legs stuck up like stripped twigs, thin and flexible.

We walked uphill towards our guesthouse. My heart sank at the row of heavily porched thirty-year-old houses. The door of the house we wanted was open and we waited in a dark hall that smelled of stale food and dust and was buzzing with flies. I was pretending to examine some sentimental prints of little girls – more permanently unreal than any Christmas card – hoping to avoid the first brush with the Misses Hortop. Brian came back from a room at the end of the hall with two quite tall and robust middle-aged ladies with perfectly white hair. They welcomed me with unprofessional nervousness made less distressing by long habit. On the whole I felt at ease with them, they were alert and sealed off from me by their own purposes – they did not strain after temporary holiday intimacy, I felt more calm at this. We were shown a pleasant bedroom overlooking the tops of trees in the valley – we were poised on the hillside and I felt exalted and breathed deeply of the cooler, fresher air from the treetops.

One day we walked a long way holding hands in silence feeling the warm rain rush at our faces and trickle off our fingers. The sky was only lightly overcast, the wet warmth filled me with a sensation of fertility. I felt a sudden rush of emotion towards the earth and the rain and the wet dungy smell of the fields, and felt a little chilled at the wet hand holding mine and at the immobile face of my partner. With the excuse to myself of my sudden rush of feeling for the day I let his hand go and ran a short way along the road, stopping at a wide gate and standing on the bottom rail to give me unnecessary inches for looking at the view. There wasn't much to see. I found from this position just a field sloping upward bordered by bushes and stunted trees whose shapes had been distorted and bent permanently inward by the power of the salt wind. One nearby corner was deeply rutted and muddy and the whole field smelt strongly of pigs. I leant over the gate and peered round to the muddy end and saw an enormous pig pushing its nose casually, erratically into the muddy grass with water streaming off its wide saddle back. It swung round and presented its bottom to me with its two large pendulant bags so obtrusive that the sight of them made me jump. I was fascinated by him, I leant over staring at the pig and his heavy bags so casually yet so all-importantly swung behind.

October 1953

I was interviewed by the headmaster of Theydon Garnon Primary School, near Epping. It's a fearsome place and he's a frightening sort of man. The school is a converted church a couple of hundred years old; a long spindly light hanging from the rafters – the walls whitewashed, the rooms made up by partitions, so that it would be easy to hear everything in the next class. It looks very grubby and cold with a little coal fire at the end of the room. Only one other infant teacher, an old woman whom the headmaster described as 'past it, without any interest in the work, so old she's always away sick.' He warned me that I'd have five or six children from a nearby Home – who are always dull and difficult to manage. Believe it or not he had other applicants for this outlandish post – so he couldn't tell me yet whether it will be 'practical' for him to employ me. He seemed extremely strict, narrow-minded and with a funny glint in his eye that I didn't trust, it looked a little unbalanced – as if he might go off the deep periodically. Well, I'm sure that's because the whole place, in the fog and dark when it was damp and cold really gave me the creeps.

November 1953

I've started supply-teaching at Epping Infants School. I've got the noisiest and most talkative class in the school, I'm told, because the teacher I'm replacing can't keep order or interest in the form. Miss Highwood (the headmistress) said she pitied me with that form, particularly as I'd never taught infants before – but she thought they wouldn't give me any trouble; she'd noticed the little regiment of girls and boys following me about the school when I first got here. They bombard you with questions and you have to run around the classroom all the time to stop them crowding out to the front. Some of them are darlings – and most of the boys want to show off like mad – even looking very hurt if I grumble at them for slinging plasticine in the girl next door's ear. One little girl won't let go of my hand and rubs her face up my arm and kisses my fingers. I feel so warm towards them I want to nurse them but that would be an unpardonable thing (the headmistress is rather a strict one). I find that if I encourage some of the most promising boys they'll do anything I ask. A little girl came up with two oval rings of plasticine with dots in the middle and said she had made my 'two big eyes.' All this and the row they kick up if you stop and relax for just a minute makes you feel as if you've done a 10 mile run when you come out – but it's exhilarating too.

December 1953
I am on Selfridges stationery counter and apart from getting in a hopeless mess over the electric cash register I don't find this job too wearing. I hate making out export forms and credit forms and getting them sanctioned or sent by post because there are so many silly forms to fill in and get signed and have bits of paper stuck on them. But apart from that the job is interesting because it's competitive. You get a commission on what you sell (at the enormous rate of

1½%!) and although this isn't much, on the counter I'm on it's possible, if you try hard, to whip up an extra pound a week. I'm not on Christmas cards, thank goodness, but on the snob counter – bridge cards, canasta, expensive leather writing cases and all the rest. It's the most envied counter on the floor because of the possibilities of good commission. I think I got picked for appearance, anyway I want to stay if that's possible. It'd be my luck to be put somewhere else tomorrow where I can't earn a halfpenny.

The girls are alright but although sweet enough at first aren't very sweet now. I took customer after customer at the beginning for nice expensive things like writing cases. I grin nicely at the men as they pass the counter and they stop and often buy. The girls, after about an hour of this, said 'Hey, who's taking all the blooming money?' – but I keep on the right side of them by being nice to them too and oh so thankful when they show me how to fill a form.

It's an amusing job because when you're tired you have a chance to play-act for the customers. I'm tactful and knowing for the elegant blue-haired ladies, cheerful with the ones who feel a bit odd, and sweet to the men, and it really does the trick. Oh well – I must do something to make it amusing, and I feel nice and secure behind my counter.

January 1954

Teaching at Chase Lane, my old infants' school. In class I had an open tussle with Miss Whitwell, the headmistress, and in prayers she told me to 'Go and stand by the wall' as if I were a child. All the teachers do their utmost to help me – particularly Miss Betty (who taught me when I was here) who says it's criminal that I'm left so entirely to my own devices with no books or paper or pencils and no constructive help, only criticism. But Whitwell's criticism doesn't in any way put me out because I've not a scrap of respect for her. Miss Betty sends round little notes saying she'll do anything to help me and giving me a few ideas and some books and magazines to cut pictures out of and stick on the wall. She has to do all this behind Whitwell's back and tells me to burn or tear up the note so that she doesn't see it!

I'm teaching a class of about forty new entrants. The kids are bedlam but I can't dislike them, they haven't a scrap of *show* about them and can't think of anything better than fighting like mad and then trying to butter me up so that I don't refuse to read a story or do something else they're interested in. They say, 'I think I'm going to be good now, Mrs Buckley,' and that lasts long enough for me to say, 'Alright then, I'll read a story,' and then they're at it again. One way and another we get on well enough and I always manage to get my own way about work.

Today Derek Dempster, who's not only a chronic pest but very dim, managed to draw a figure four for me, after I'd been with him about ten minutes, and I praised him so much and said so many times how clever he was that when I was telling him off (as I am every two seconds) and made him sit next to me while I read the story, as I took his hand away from my book he kissed mine – and made me feel very very fond of him. Coming from him that really means something as far as his wanting to do things I ask him to do is concerned – because he alone could drive you mad if he felt like it.

February 1954

One dark-haired girl and a rather sturdy little boy in the class have become smitten with each other and every so often they face and cuddle each other, and the little boy plays with the buttons on her jumper and puts his hands across her chest. Then he gently runs his hands up her leg and she sits there smiling sweetly with her legs apart. Neither of them seem a bit curious or shy, they just look at each other and smile. I'm very gentle with them when I tell them to sit still and pay attention, I hardly like to say anything to them except that if I let them carry on the other kids would never stop laughing or giggling. I come over all warm with affection for them and want to smile at them all day.

Today it's been damned hard – the kids were noisier as well because nosy-poking Whitwell has been in and out like a Jack-in-the-box and that makes them hard to handle. Great fat Miss Appleton sat next to me at dinner and put her blooming great arms in my dinner about five times so that it was all I could do to eat it. It's a fulltime job passing her more potatoes, more meat, more greens, more gravy – more, more, I don't know where the devil she puts it all.

One of my devotees, Alan Hastings, a precocious only son of middle-aged parents, whenever he comes out to tell a story always begins by talking to the class – gently and firmly telling them to be quiet and stop fidgeting before he begins – using all the words I use and the manner in which I say them; and afterwards he says 'I want to ask them questions about it' – so I let him ask a few.

March 1954

Today the kids worked hard because the sun has been shining and they were full of beans. I went to see Whitwell for some counters for them and talked to her a little and she seemed very mild. She has been quite decent to me lately, saying 'You really have them where you want them now, haven't you?' and she even allowed me to insist that they were ready for some reading books without that look of *What are you talking about* in her eyes.

Playground duty is quite funny when I have one kid to each finger (not all of them from my class) and those who haven't got a finger hang on to my coat and I have to say which way I want to turn so that I can get the little crowd to turn at the same time, or else I just tug myself free and they start fighting each other to get back.

This evening the tank burst in the secretary's room and it was all flooded out with water pouring from the ceiling. Whitwell opened the door and had a fit – 'Oh, all the paper and stock and typewriter – somebody get it out.' No-one did anything, least of all Whitwell, so I just nipped through and started handing it all out. Whitwell was like a big hen clucking about and taking the things from me and saying all the time, 'Don't get wet, Mrs Buckley, don't get wet' and I was just perched on my toes in the pond with bits of wet hair sticking round my face.

May 1954

Second term teaching. It's strange I don't seem to notice it much. Certainly I don't worry in the least – not a bit as it used to be – I never come to grips sufficiently for it to be gruelling now.

I had a first class tiff with a mother yesterday which ended very quickly because I was extremely short-tempered with her and she went away red as a beetroot and smouldering with annoyance and embarrassment with the way I spoke to her. I had no intention of being abrupt but she was very rude and I lost my temper. Her boy had been fighting and wouldn't stop – I smacked him, he was a spoilt weak kid and sat whimpering all the time. His mum came up to me and said 'He says he had a smack – is that the way to make him like school?' Without thinking I went for her – and she went away so resentfully, I thought she'd probably try to make a fuss with Whitwell. But I'm not even faintly worried – the whole lot of them can go to the devil.

And Miss Whitwell sticks up for me nicely now. When the mother complained to her, Whitwell told her not to be so silly and that if she had any complaint to make it was that I was *too* kind and easy with the children.

Spring 1955

Interview at Dagenham Grammar School. I got the job and afterwards was taken to meet the Head of the English department. He was hanging out of an open window on the first floor yelling like a drunkard at some boys outside walking on the edge of the low hedged wall that runs along the front of the school.

The noise was deafening – I felt shattered and unable to grasp the situation. The voice was so charged with emotion I thought he must be going to scream or burst into tears or throw a fit. After a while it ceased and he turned round and came towards me. I searched his face to see if he were recovered, but it only offered a grimace of bored welcome:

'So you're the new one, how d'you do?' He held my hand hotly and limply for a split second and let it go with apparent disgust. I was mortified and felt myself beginning to blush.

Mrs Ramsey, the secretary, said jollily that she'd leave us to it and went out, shutting the metal-framed door noisily behind her.

'Well, sit down, Miss – er –'

'Ramsey – I mean Buckley.'

'How do you like the look of the school?'

'Well, I've not seen very much of it – only the rooms in the old building where I was interviewed – and these few classrooms. I've not seen any of the children yet.'

'Oh, you didn't come to lunch then before the interview – pity – it's always best to get a taster before you commit yourself. Still, it's not a bad place; plenty of light and air.'

'The children?'

'They're alright when you get used to them – some of them need a firm hand though – can you be firm?'

'I think so, I'm pretty sure I can – I don't like to be beaten.'

'That's the spirit!' He sounded both sceptical and indifferent.

I wanted to make this man behave more friendlily: after all, he was going to be a colleague, wasn't he? 'Do you like it here?'

He looked shocked and put his thin lips out and in several times and blinked. 'I've been here ten years so I suppose I must.'

I was beginning to dislike him heartily – was this the way to welcome a new member of staff? I had expected some sort of general encouragement – 'We're not a bad lot really' or 'You'll soon settle down, the staffroom's a friendly, homely place' – anything, lies or not, was better than this – he was treating me as if he resented me and was contemptuous of me for taking the job.

'I'm not going to bother you with details of the syllabus now, I'll send you a copy a week or two before term starts – and your timetable, which hasn't been worked out yet. Incidentally, I think you'll probably have to take 3C – Mr Wilkes has been taking them for the past two years and refuses to take them again. The others have got their hands full so you'll have them, I should say.'

I said nothing, I felt miserable with misgivings – I was dying to ask him why Mr Wilkes had refused but I didn't have the courage.

'I'll try and work in a couple of A forms for you but there are four fulltime English staff with you, and you're the junior, so you see how things are.'

I nodded without enthusiasm.

'I'll take you along to see the English store and show you where things are so you won't be lost on the first day. Anything you want to ask before we go?'

I knew there must be dozens of things but I couldn't think of any – I didn't really know what I'd need to know until I'd started teaching. 'I don't think so,' I said.

'Righto.' We walked briskly down the corridor, went down some stairs and turned left into a little dead-end of rooms. Right at the end was the English store room. He unlocked the door and pointed to one shelf after another quickly – first year, second year, third year and so on. 'You'll know what texts you'll be taking with each class when you get your timetable.'

The mass of untidy books in front of me made me feel sick, so did the smell of ink and dirt that came from them.

'Any questions?'

'No.'

He shut the door and we went on down the stairs. 'Well, if there's nothing else I can do for you I'll be off – got a load of marking to do – didn't finish till ten last night! Good luck!' He was off.

Good God, what an awful man! Were they all like this, or was he just extremely tired and overworked?

Spring 1957

I haven't really stopped thinking, but I'm no longer intoxicated by the fabrication of ideas born of other ideas where the original connection with a living problem is left far behind and only the flattery of the name of thought left. Thinking purposefully about one's experience is necessary and if one is living a full life to some extent inevitable. Thinking for the sake of thinking, keeping the intellectual motor in tiptop condition by continual overhauls and trial runs is not. I see the intellect as a mechanical thing that one keeps bright and spruce to show off with – just like a car. But not the intelligence – that grows as your life grows and is full if your life is full. One can be very brilliant and entertaining and have a stunted intelligence. Brian and I want the whole of life – and that's something you don't get if you are not willing to give yourself up to the parts. You don't get anything by holding yourself in reserve for what you might mistakenly think are your big aims in life. That way you miss all the important things. You'd never know what was important and what wasn't – how could you, you wouldn't have tried the variety of experience necessary to make a fair judgment.

October 1959

Since Jane was born I've forgotten what it was like to be a single self. This has produced a great contempt for the 'old self.' Where is all the pride and the mastery and the intellect and the determination? – disappeared as if it were all a kid's game made up to stand in the place of real events until you should be old enough to experience them.

I have been in some way humbled, not cringing but less assertive of my rights. It's as if I've been relieved of carrying around the burden of a constantly irascible sense of my own rights as a human being – the singularity that produced the attitude has been dispersed.

If you want anything outside yourself – that is if you really deeply let yourself want something outside yourself – you lose your identity to some extent, you're changed. Isn't that what we all want – isn't that what love is all about – and children – and childbirth – it's all a passing on – out of yourself through and with others. I can't imagine anyone wanting a congealed, stillborn identity.

I feel I want to discard the old anxieties, the old need to impress myself upon other people, to keep tapping out the nervous morse of communication between alien existences.

December 1959

When I go to see Brian's mother, who is seriously ill, I am filled with compassion for her. I would go with Brian whenever he goes which would give us an opportunity to share the wretchedness of seeing her like that but Jane has to be fed five times a day and I cannot always be free. We are living here as if we have both been injected with some appalling drug that brings about a leaden and wearying indifference fraught with self-accusation and causes us not to recognise each other but to drag through each day on our own.

The one clear shaft of joy there is at this time is our daughter; at least, that's what she is for me. She is so warm, sweet, full of life and enchanting mannerisms, dewy fresh and completely lovable. My father manifests the same heart-rending slavishness towards her as he must have done to me – so obviously begging and so exposed to betrayal – it's difficult to sort out the pity from the anger and the feeling of self-righteousness from the feeling of guilt towards him.

September 1962

My nauseous Kenilworth neighbours are at this moment screeching at each other across our garden, congratulating each other on their progress and how hard they have worked. Brian has worked extremely hard but because we have spent nothing on outside help we are regarded as being very slow and slothful. In any normal sane-living community it would not be expected that one have one's garden in Ideal Home condition within the first year, but in this place the pressure is appalling. Next time we'll buy a field with *no* immediate neighbours, we promise ourselves this luxury – we don't mind how much we cut down on the house for the freedom of living on our own.

I have made 30 lbs of jam and marmalade this week (damson, plum, grapefruit and lemon) planted twenty winter cabbages and am hoping to help get the grass laid in the early part of next week. After this the next job is to redecorate the kitchen. I feel I must plunge myself up to the neck in work. It provides a personal intensity of life that is a very poor substitute for beauty, freedom, health, relaxed living – general joy.

It is now Monday. We worked hard in the garden over the weekend and Brian caught up with his study programme for three hours every evening. Instead of my spirits changing quickly with changing weather and changing interests I seem to get more gloomy every day. Perhaps it's because of this perishing sore throat which seems to be nearly throttling me today. I feel a wreck; I also feel that if I make up I look like 'a jazzed up old hag' rather than just a tired one – so I hold off from doing so most of the time as the sight of myself in the mirror disgusts me. It seems such a far cry from a few months ago when I had complete and unshakeable pride and self-assurance in my body and appearance. I find it difficult to understand why Brian still wants me. One always feels that conditions like this are permanent – it's very difficult to get a scrap of comfort from the thought that in a few weeks (or days?) time one might not feel like this, because all one can feel is that one *might*.

I feel as if I haven't seen a soul in months. In fact it's only just over a week since we came back from our holiday in Cornwall, and since then we have been invited out 3 times – but I feel as if I haven't left the house. I didn't want and didn't really enjoy any of these encounters – they were more than I could manage – I can't seem to face people nowadays, I don't want anything to do with them.

Brian keeps asking why I don't fix up a meeting, now Jenny's recovered from her cold (all bar catarrh) with the usual clique of child-owners on this estate, but the thought appals me – I'd rather curl in on myself in embryonic fashion. These casual, empty-headed, moderately efficient, permanently busy females would be enough to make me shoot myself, if I had a gun.

October 1962

I'm struggling to be different, not depressed, without hope, without philosophy, without life – but it's a struggle. I haven't the faintest idea why I should feel as if each day tends to be a little more pointless than the last – but there it is. I no longer feel lethargic and passive about it – but venomous. It could be that my spirits aren't in good shape because their carcase isn't.

I've just lost my last cold and am sickening for another – a sore throat like little men tramping up and down it with those spiked mountain boots on. Brian threatens me with another day in bed tomorrow if it hasn't gone by then (this is its second day) – and how I loathe the inside of that bloody bed during the daytime, I could set fire to it. Jane seems well, thank the Lord, but 10 to 1 she'll catch it if I can't arrest this one in midstream. She'll probably catch it anyway.

Forget it.

Something momentarily, temporarily, but quite successfully gay-making is the garden. Like the fiercely enthusiastic slob I am, because seeding is now impossible because it's too bloody late and too bloody cold and rainstorms are constantly sending other people's seeds in torrents down the hillside on which we live, and we have seen them in sackcloth and ashes wringing their hands over their washed out hordes, I have decided we must turf the lot and *now*. I'm sick to death of looking out on a churned up building site and want some semblance of greenery and life. And our neighbours say, 'And so say all of us,' because of course their gardens have been for the past six months positive masses of bloom and greenery and they feel, 'Now everyone seems to be putting their backs into it, it (the estate) is going to be quite nice.' I am going to plant a tree on the front lawn with two trunks branching out from the same root so that it looks something like a V sign.

So last week we ordered 120 sq. yds of turf and with back-breaking endeavour laid it all on the back lawn – what a delicious change that two days of murderous muscle ache has made. Mrs Cullum next door is delighted. The only trouble is that she has fenced us in so far up her side of the garden to hide from her sensitive eyes the monstrous deformity of our back yard that now she entirely misses the benefit of its greenery. All she can see now is our huge vegetable patch. More pain....

Now while I am still working like a black preparing the land (fabulously hardworking, me recently, lots of pies and large cooked meals, fanatical regularity and efficiency in housework, washing and ironing etc and whenever there is a moment to spare, with sweat pouring from my brow I dig, shape, level, prepare land and lay turf – a true wife and worker at last) Brian is off on the Glory Road again. He has decided that for the next ten months or so he must work every evening and every weekend in bringing his lecture on *Women in Love* up to publishable standard. So my temporary enthusiasm is snapped in two prematurely and becomes an isolated, will-inflicted endurance test. I shouldn't be surprised if the front lawn remains half laid throughout the winter with piles of rotting turf in one corner of it. I shall have to take up some eccentric occupation in the evenings like basket-making or whoring or something....

We bought a wooden gate and I made a fence with 10 shillings worth of sawn wood that I nailed on to batons. I hammered at the wall and plugged it with wood in preparation for the gate post so that all Brian had to do was to knock 5 inch nails through post and wall to fix it to it, which I couldn't manage. Then for the other gate post I had to chip at the corner of the paving stone for a whole morning like a convict in order to get a neat square corner off and not break or chip the rest of it; and then underneath I found two bricks which had to receive the same treatment, and it took a *long long* time. And when the hole was ready Brian put the concrete in and the post. Then we swung the gate together. Then I hammered up my home-made fence and creosoted all. It looks very good; and creosoted the trellis.

Even while I was creosoting my fence our neighbour Mrs Cullum came out and tore me off a strip for the choice of latrine my cat has made. She has a strip of earth between our two houses she chooses to leave bare and to plant shrubs in. Naturally the cat uses it. She says she won't do a thing with it, she'll just leave it, that animals ought not to be allowed in open-planned estates (as if *anything* stops a cat) and I ought to take the cat out on a lead and so on. I told her that I've never heard of anyone being held morally responsible for their cats' sanitary arrangements. I said I was sorry but I failed to see what I could do about it as I did not intend to take him out on a lead (there are five other cats to my knowledge on this small estate). It is the fact that he is so young makes him a little perisher. He'll settle down in a month or two. And I was busy putting up my fence at that very time to keep my livestock in as much as possible. I must admit, to my shame and anger, that when I got indoors I burst into tears. These neighbours depress and demoralise me. They live incarcerated in property-righteousness and sterile hygiene. 'I bath, therefore I am,' as I heard in a play the other night.

I have been much more cheerful since Mum and Dad arrived – but their therapeutic effect is beginning to fail – after all they are Mum and Dad, however fond you are of them, and the possibilities of communication are severely limited. I took great pleasure in dressing them up like dear big dolls. Dad has a new coat and Mum a new coat and hat, I forced them upon them both (the choice that is) but they are now terribly pleased with them. (Mummy is an absolute nut about what suits her: likes coats with fur collars, which look awful on her – she looks like a snowman with no neck in them and yet gravitates towards them like a child towards lollipops.) I insisted on her having a hat to suit the coat and set it off instead of one of those Woolworth's buns she always wears. I have great difficulty in persuading her to wear it properly and with dignity to bring warmth into her face and bring out the colour of her coat – she slyly tips it back and cocks it on to one side given a chance, like some silly little London sparrow. Not that I really care of course, it's a game with me. I pretend to mind because it pleases her to think I do. If she wants to wear it upside down, that's her affair. They are both the sweetest parents.

November 1962
Dull wet – endless weather-consciousness – a smokiness about all the days. Jane with an allergy that won't go away (spots in patches on her) and me with a period that won't arrive. I feel walled in, shut up in myself and my house, constipated in all my feelings and with an endless underlying craving to be able to live again. This is partly due to all the construction work I've been doing: the work that seems to be of vital necessity to me and yet exhausts me and makes

my world even smaller and more insular. The work and the exhaustion are private, non-communicated, and the circle closes in and in.

Brian has been immersing me head first into a little cesspool of tepid female society. I have two or three around a week, generally they have children (not particularly suited to Jane in age or any other way) or are pregnant. Brian thinks no matter how much I hate or despise these women I ought to have some outside contacts – else my tongue cleaves to the roof of my mouth and my eyes stare and see nothing. In a way unpleasant society is preferable to none, in as much as it at least sets in motion the wheels of response to an immediate situation: you know you can still respond. Otherwise it is imprisonment of tongue and thought and feeling, until the blissful evenings when Brian is home. Not that I don't relish and appreciate Jane – she's in every way adorable – it's just that, while Brian is out at work, two thirds of the rest of my being are left over, spare, wasted, bored – and living here in the flat and foggy Midlands I feel disoriented.

I decided to take Jane into Coventry to see the Toy Fair. I started by keeping her away from everyone – drawing her in close to me because this person looked so pale, that one held his throat, the other suggested disease in his very walk. In fact they were just town-dwellers. My horror of them, of their life, took the form of feeling it to be in some way contaminating. The afternoon was abject. It began in a ghastly twilight of damp smoke and ended in night at about 4.30. After we had seen a tawdry exhibition of Hong Kong clockwork toys we came home in a bus smelling like a zoo – grease, sweat, staleness, captivity, exhaustion of will. Jane and I, I fancied, were from a different planet and we (I) were afraid of being insulted, jeered at, afraid of having to say two words to the coarse insulting Irish conductress, and filled with murderous loathing of the dirty-haired working zombie who turned round and addressed no-one with 'Stop kicking the seat please.' Jane had just started to tap the seat in front and I had just put my hand on her leg to stop her and opened my mouth to reprove her. One is powerless in such a place. I wanted to hide or wished for a miracle that would suddenly open up for me green fields and us walking home through them with fine air to breathe.

Coming home, our house was warm, welcoming, separated from that place in its appearance but devastatingly smug and self-conscious, lined up with all the other pricey houses and bungalows on this so-select little estate. It looks like property – I've never had a home that looked like property before: I hate that aspect of it. Inside it's home alright – our mess and inefficiency inside, I feel at ease in it mostly – in the lounge I feel perfectly at home. But how awful when the sense of comfort and freedom belongs to a couple of rooms.

January 1963
I feel as if my blood is flowing like ice – like this incredible white iron imprisonment we are subjected to in this forsaken place. For more than three weeks now I have been unwell. I had a course of penicillin which didn't work, then a course of chloromycetin which seems to have set me well on the road to recovery but I am chafing at the bit because I'm not

there yet. I can't keep my lower regions warm – I wear tights, three pairs of knickers and an altered woolly jumper all around my bottom – I look quite gross and shapeless around my backside – but even that is not enough – whenever I go out into these polar conditions, so the backache and bladder pains start up and the pain of urinating. For a long time I drank as much as two pints of water an hour – how abominable it is to keep on drinking and drinking! At the two pints an hour rate it is like a form of torture: I was desperate to get rid of it. In addition to this my ankles are weak and often hurt: I don't yet know whether this is part of the complaint or whether it is an entirely separate effect of the cold. The doctor has now put me on one large tablet a day for the next fifteen days and we'll see how far I get with that. I hate the whole bloody business; if I do too much housework (and I never really do much) I get the pains back: as well as through excessive cold. The temperature here has been below freezing for weeks: for a few days about half a week ago it came to just above freezing point but now it is well below it again and 'snow is frozen snow on snow, snow on snow.' If you stick a spade in the 20 inches of snow in our garden it stands up like poker because it is so hard – I can't even get a spade in.

This white hard world is hateful and annihilating. And tomorrow Brian starts work: and for the whole holiday I have been ill so we've had no good times together, I've hardly set foot outside the house, we can't even make love because of the disease being in the wrong zone, making me very tender. And this term Brian is on school-practice supervision again so his

hours of work are increased again. I am so full of self-
pity I spend many of these days on the verge of tears –
for no good reason at all – just a piece of music, a
chance remark or thought.

February 1963
Jane was pale, abstracted, drooping, complaining of
pains in her throat: I took her to the doctor's on
Friday. She had a virus infection of the throat and
glands and he gave her the same antibiotic medicine
she had had just a couple of weeks before for her ears.
So we dosed her up again and she developed the most
appalling fluey cold I have ever seen – I have never
seen eyes and nose stream so constantly, endlessly,
day after day – it was so bad that I had to put Vaseline
on her nose and lips every half hour and then that
didn't stop them from cracking open and bleeding, the
stream of liquid was too much for the skin. In the
mornings the mucous and blood on her face formed a
solid 'concrete' surface so that she couldn't smile or
talk without pain until it was cleared away – it was
even set hard on her teeth. Meantime the throat pains
died away under the influence of the medicine. On
Sunday I had to go to bed with vicious throat pains
and these developed in expected fashion to headache,
earache, pains in the limbs – incredible tiredness, for
the first few days I wanted to sleep practically all day
as well as all night – and of course, with me, gastritis
with it. I refrained from calling in the doctor for the
first two days thinking I could manage, but when on
the third day the throat was still bad (it prevents you
from sleeping continuously – you must have some
soothing pastille in your mouth all the night) I called

him, which was very fortunate and well-timed because Jane had been recovering from her fluey symptoms slowly and I had heard no more complaints about the throat since Friday and then suddenly she went quite white again and dark under the eyes and complained of pains in her throat and ears. So when the doctor came I wanted him to see her more than me and believe it or not I had given the bloody throat infection back to her. He has given her a much stronger 'killer' drug rather than a 'suppressive' (which is what she had before) and that seems to have made a marked and quick improvement. She is very jolly today even though her glands are still swollen. She has eaten well too. He has given me some antibiotic tablets too and says he will call and see her again on Thursday or Friday and that in any case we can't go out until then, so we must just wait for him.

April 1963
Mrs Watkins made the house *exquisite* when we came home from our Cornish holiday: she is wonderful. She had scrubbed my two bedroom armchairs, polished and cleaned and washed everywhere. She had put a wonderful display of forsythia in the lounge and had brought me (from her own plants) two pots of indoor begonias; the boiler was on and the bottle was in our bed. She had worked for five hours without break or meal on the Thursday of our return. (Oh! she also cleaned out my broom and rag and saucepan cupboard – it had been in an *awful* state – and took home a dozen dusters and bits of rag and washed them and brought them back for cleaning.) She seems to have a very real motherly affection for us all and does her

work terribly well and thoroughly. I feel very spoilt really, all things considered.

I've just interrupted Jane and her pal Melanie from inspecting each other's bottoms: they said coming out of the loo, 'Can we see each other's bottoms?' I sounded surprised yet didn't want to make anything of it so I said, 'Well, you've seen them before' – they said 'Only once' – so I made some silly excuse about them getting cold etc and left them for about two minutes and then came back insisting that that was enough as they'd catch cold and suggested they play in the garden. How's that for cowardice? 'Plenty of fresh air and healthy exercise' was my solution: ever heard that before? Every hateful P.T. and games bod has the same idea, eh? – or should it be Ugh! I don't want to stop healthy natural curiosity or give them any reason whatever to feel it's something to be secretive about, however I had to interfere: Lord knows why: general stinking background, civilization and all the rest of it, I suppose.

June 1963
Nancy Young is a 32-year-old student who has been throwing herself like a ton of bricks at Brian. I read an essay of hers and asked Brian to ask her and her husband home because she was lively and intelligent it seemed from her work. After the second or third meeting I found it necessary to cut across her line of attack on Brian and it drew her off on to me – she buttonholed me on all occasions and talked intently into my face, walking at an incredible rate. It promised a fairly interesting friendship – at least we could talk to each other without having to reduce

everything to children, housework and words of one syllable. Her husband meanwhile, a tall, thin, apparently uncouth architect (one of the very few, according to himself, who has a degree in the subject – I didn't know there was one) remained a quiet nonentity in the background whenever we met as a foursome. Slowly however he has come to life as a somewhat electric idealist who has already committed adultery once and makes it very obvious he would be delighted to do so again. However he is not a lecher, he is extremely rarefied – passionately fond of music and in particular Bach. Fond of the geometric and linear in architecture – black and white – purist but hysterical fundamentally and extremely passionate. In consequence the rather harsh angular friendship that was growing up between Nancy and myself has been reduced to a nagging observation and constant reiteration to me of the misery her husband has caused her. She has become impossible – she no longer appears to be very intelligent even (though she is the only woman in the college to have received four A's – one in each subject).

Frank and I are extremely reluctant to engage in any warfare of the sexes; this is putting it mildly: I have a horror of it – but he has a coldly passionate, incisive, hysterical, easily depressed easily elated relationship with me that is wearing, exhausting but stirring and provoking. He has left a whole pile of records with us and wants me to listen to some in particular – and the music is stirring and establishes a relationship which I don't want to be there. Last time they were here Brian rowed with him for most of the evening because of the hysterical way he was showing off – positively performing for my benefit, and I was blushing and laughing and responding and only afterwards regretting it. In the middle of the performance he trots out a Biblical quotation with his finger pointing at me that makes me run cold: 'He that lusts after a woman in his heart has already committed adultery with the woman.'

Things will subside and be normal again soon, because that's the way *I will have it.* Nobody wants any more pain, what the hell it's only lust, I don't love anyone but Brian and never could. It's all a childish game which must cease.

July 1963
We have all been going through a rather dark and abstract patch. Jane has been unwell – catarrhal congestion around the ears, and bad teeth. She is recovering quite well from the former and I'm taking her to the dentist tomorrow about the latter. She has been confined indoors for three days but the doctor says she should be alright to travel by midweek. I am waiting for a period to start – thickened in every fibre and a bit sentimental and melancholic. Lastly – and probably the main cause of our temporary painful stoniness – we have set ourselves the most fantastic gardening feat to be accomplished before our Cornish holiday – the latter goal being the incentive and reward: be good girls and boys and you get a sweetie; only we have to arrange a little bit of 'nasty' to come just before the 'sweetie' in order to keep our moral education happy. Our garden has been a jungle of weeds and our one-fifth of a wall has helped to increase the general appearance of ruin and collapse.

We have designed a lawn stretching out from house and from side fence to side fence; a semicircular flowerbed beyond it; a Cotswold stone wall and a shrubbery above and behind it; and a five-foot grass verge around three sides of the shrubbery. The general appearance is spacious and dignified – easy and peaceful to look at as opposed to the 'fuss' around us. Brian has heaved a *ton and a half* of stone up 20 steps that are precipitously steep and has weeded and altered the entire level of the flower border which has entailed digging up all the plants, heaving loads of earth on to the shrubbery and then replanting them – and burying sand not wanted, and in this way exposed, in same shrubbery. I've finished the wall. We have to take it in shifts: mornings I stay in with Jane and do housework and cooking etc while Brian does four hours gardening; afternoons I go out, he stays in with Jane.

September 1963

After our lovely time in Cornwall we have had re-initiation all round this last week. Brian to lecturing again and entirely new faces on all fronts – his students change completely each year: disconcerting in a way: refreshing if you've had a poor crowd. Jane starting back to nursery school after nine or ten weeks off and no Melanie to go with and 17 new faces in her class – all the rest have gone up, being a year older than her; only one face she knows and likes. Anyway the new children will be roughly her age – although she'll still be one of the youngest, being only just four. She screamed for a solid hour the first morning, the headmistress had to come in and intimidate her:

she wouldn't let anyone touch her or come near her to comfort her – she kept far away from them all and had her bit of hysteria. I was greeted by red puffy eyes at 12.15. The next morning after a cold lecture from me there were a few tears that didn't last very long and since then it has got progressively better. She even managed a little smile the other morning and today I saw her busying herself with the others when I left. It would have been no use giving in to her: all her friends are at school – she'd have no-one to play with and she goes potty and 'spotty' at home with boredom, so there we are. Her eczema is still improving with the calamine treatment, so I haven't taken her to the doctor's on this occasion.

My re-initiation has been into housework: endless washing and ironing and cooking and cleaning and entertaining students etc. I've got the lounge to start on this weekend or next. We've bought all the paint and paper; we're just waiting for the energy.

The new lecturer, Matthew Crompton, whom Brian was interested in on sight when he was appointed turns out to be *really* interesting. We had them round one evening and found that we spoke the same language (hardly surprising as all four of us had English degrees: the first couple we have met who had the same degrees as each other). They are unaffected, honest (it would seem) roughly the same background as ourselves and he is certainly intelligent. One can't tell about Angela, she is very quiet; he on the other hand is explosive, passionate, talkative, funny, a little clownish: gesticulates constantly. He is good-looking with his steel-grey hair and obviously young and lively face and large eyes. He has a passion for television but doesn't own one, so they'll probably be coming round to see the international film on Friday, *Il bel Antonio*; the wife, being a cooler subject altogether, doesn't find so much interest in it. He has a fascinating way of dressing himself. Obviously the clothes allowance goes on him. She was wearing a skirt and jumper she could have had from college days, he was wearing a fantastic rigout, American-type shirt, buttoned-down collar, in blue check, a blue-black-grey striped jacket (broadish bands of colour) and very tight black trousers, black socks with bars of thin gold and 'Teddy shoes,' smooth all over the top and pointed as hell. On top of all this was a Barry Foster hair cut: you'd notice him in a crowd. Strangely enough the general effect instead of being ludicrous was flattering, he's very conscious of his appearance and makes the best of it, however superficially odd or flashy this would seem to lead him to be.

I am intrigued by Angela, she seems to be intelligent in a depressed sort of way – not temperamentally but conditionally: I don't suppose she gets the urge to 'bubble' much with him around. She watches and notices things; smiles quite easily and would seem to have an affectionate streak; not enemies at first glance anyway – willing to be friendly without, at the moment, a trace of cattiness. Matthew buys her clothes or 'dresses' her as she says – and he dresses her as near as he can like a man. Stripes, heavy allover sweaters, trousers, shapeless dresses – many shirts actually bought in a man's shop. She is very very lean but when dressed in a black shapeless dress she looks more feminine than usual and suggests a dispassionate, rather lascivious sexiness.

With it all there is an odd kind of innocence and tenderness about them that would seem to deny all this but nevertheless doesn't. They are frank to the point of exhibitionism.

October 1963

This feeling is eating me up – I must get it off my chest. I am likely to sound a little incoherent and a little melodramatic, I'm dead tired, I've been going out every night and weekends for ages but last night laid me low. I don't seem to have domestic time with Brian any more to balance me up and I go berserk without it. I woke up with a painful stomach at 4 o'clock this morning with pains in my nether regions; at six o'clock I woke up again and burst into tears that ran like water – not altogether relieving. At 9.30 I was singing elatedly taking Jane to school walking in the brisk clear marvellous autumn sunshine, and now I'm back on the verge of tears again. What am I to do? I fall in love as easily as some people catch flu.

Last week was the first time we have seen Nancy and Frank since we came back from Cornwall: it was about 8 or 9 weeks without seeing them. I've been putting it off and putting it off and in spite of my reluctance to see them again have become increasingly restless and depressed because of it: hence the constant going out and busy social life. We went round to supper with them. I've honestly thought of very little else for days since then: not exactly constantly, but the thought of him has threaded itself through almost everything. He's a difficult and tough and independent bastard. There's none of the clinging mellowness, that acolyte dependence and service of the spirit that wrung me so before. Sometimes I am convinced that we dislike each other.

The evening was monstrous. Bloody hawk-eye Nancy, always at the watch, makes it impossible to let a true emotion be read in my face: I always cover up with snappiness and curtness and rudeness to him: it's becoming so much of a habit that I've almost forgotten how else to behave. I flaunt my liking of other men: say how attractive I find them: I can see he dislikes this: he returns this in kind with a little extra for good measure – we bicker, disagree on almost everything we talk about, we aren't allowed to talk about any of the easy sociable subjects because they bore him: we are forced into high moral planes almost immediately when our feelings are anything but 'highly moral.' Not that he is hypocritical, far from it – I admire his attitude in some fields, in others I find it miserably cynical, cold, angular. I think that the one thing I find so difficult to handle in this case is that he is intelligent, strong-minded and independent – not the right, not the easy qualities for an object of love to have; I mean of course when that object is not legitimately allowed to respond to you naturally as my husband can.

Throughout these patches there are smooth, balmy flows of peace and almost tenderness between us. He is extremely knowledgeable and sensitive about music. I'm not glamorising him here – as Brian has admitted, Frank is one of the few people we have met who have added to our experience – not just in architecture, where I feel his tastes (and so does

Brian) to be admirably purist, but in music where I am
already a little knowledgeable myself and can
appreciate the extent of his response and knowledge.
He points out new music, music I've never listened to
because it required too much effort, and tells me what
to look for. This is an intellectual and emotional
adventure: the last Beethoven quartets, Bach's
unaccompanied cello music, and so on – which I find
after three or four listenings fantastically good – and
Brian too. Reading a score while the music is being
played is also wonderfully rewarding. One can see the
themes and patterns moving from one part to the next
and being inverted and adapted: somehow you can
hear *all* the parts at once and it is wonderfully exciting
and fulfilling.

In one of our peaceful moments he showed me how
to read a score to the 3rd and 6th Brandenburg
concertos. He stood behind my chair with his arms
holding up the score for me – both arms round my
neck but not touching me – I was terrified that the
radiance I felt would be there in my face and to my
grief I saw Brian looking tense and caught up in
himself with his face turned away. Frank's finger
pointed out the quickly changing, weaving, turning,
subtle light patterns of music, the pages flipping over
rapidly as if I were eating the score hungrily.

I can't help but love him – he is fiercely alive. I
don't think I love him very much, only appreciatively.
If natural reactions weren't forbidden between
members of the opposite sex who are married, would
we feel free to be simply very good friends? It's all
this bloody feeling of guilt that turns it into something
else.

My reaction to Frank in no way means that I intend to carry on to the obvious conclusion. Quite the contrary – I've had enough of all that: through and through – saturated with the hatefulness of it – and it is this that prevents me ever allowing myself to get closer to him. I'm more armoured with bands of steel from an instinctive loathing of the whole business (above all the pain it would inflict on the one person I love beyond everything) than all my reasoning about it could ever hope to make me. I *cannot* let myself go in his presence – I feel as if I'm gripped by something that I have no control over whatever – even when I want him to touch me. Twice he has moved towards an embrace and twice I've shut up like a clam – been cold and nasty – just turned away, giving the impression that 'really this is absurd;' and so he makes his communication through music and in this I let myself go.

The most I have ever allowed myself with Frank is in response to a passionate look. When we were alone on one occasion he looked at me with keen, utterly open love. He was sitting and looking up at me – perhaps because of the position it was intensely intimate and expressive of love. I gave back the look and moved nearer to him, but then Brian came in.

November 1963
We invited all our new friends to a party. I spent days preparing food and cocktaily-type snacks and trifles and cakes and biscuits and so on; we spent lots on booze (all added to our overdraft) and two other people brought a bottle of wine with them in spite of the fact that we told them all not to. So everyone got

thoroughly drunk (there were ten of us and we provided for a bottle and a half each). Matthew didn't bring his car because he knew he wouldn't be able to drive back. He apparently fell asleep as soon as he got home (he didn't leave until 3.30 a.m.) and an hour later found himself running towards the bathroom being violently sick on the way. He said he managed to get vomit on both walls so it must have been coming out of his ears!

They all professed to have enjoyed themselves wonderfully – 'Marvellous party – wish you'd do it more often' and so on. But they were all so bloody drunk they wouldn't have known if it was a good party or not. Myself, I was thoroughly and utterly disgusted and depressed most of the time, not by other people but by myself. I was so fantastically nervous that I couldn't hold a cigarette still, it wobbled about all over the place like a comedy performance. In consequence to calm myself down I got stone drunk within the first three quarters of an hour. By the time the later guests arrived I was finding it difficult to manage the stairs or to pour wine without spilling it all over their hands and cuffs. Everyone was marvellously gay and cheerful, there was jiving downstairs and lounging upstairs. Matthew was worth his weight in gold as a catalyst. He was a little star performer flitting from one guest to the next being witty, bawdy, intimate. The more I saw things were going smoothly without my interference the more I realised how agonisingly drunk I was – I couldn't see properly – about all I could do was jive. When Matthew and I were dancing I apologised for not being able to jive at all and our dance consisted entirely of his thrusting me away from him fiercely and then equally fiercely and quickly making our bodies touch and then thrust away again and then touch again. I thought it was a pretty crumby dance and apologised and he said 'Nonsense, you're doing fine, it's terribly sexy!' – which is the last thing in the world I would have called it.

All the time I felt this unspeakable disgust of myself. Angela seemed to be the closest and nearest most of the time – sweet and kind and understanding. Anyway, she tidied my appearance when my dress slipped down off my shoulder from the exertions of dancing, saying that my 'pretty white shoulder' was showing, and cuddled me in the intervals, and then when I decided to go to sleep on the stairs she helped me up to the bedroom and sat with me a long while comforting and cuddling me and caressing my side and arms and making me feel very relaxed and communicative. I decided she was a friendly and affectionate soul, and at the same time shrewd and cool and very well aware of what was going on – pumped me for information about my relationships with men and so on. That may sound a little sinister but I don't think it was, she pleasantly surprised me – I was very grateful for her kindness and sympathy.

The Youngs were at the party – Nancy showed a will to battle with her dislike of me, Frank showed a will to battle with the opposite. I have since relieved them both of the burden of the necessity (and myself incidentally) by telling Brian all. He was marvellous. I'm now going through a period of slow depression at having completely thrown over Frank Young – but essentially, I suppose, relieved. I still find the man the most interesting and exciting and certainly the most intelligent of all our acquaintances: but more remotely now, I seem to have driven in the final wedge between us.

December 1963
We're *always* out three evenings a week, sometimes four or five. We've just cancelled the fourth evening for this week because I can't take going to bed at one or one-thirty any longer. We have the play-reading club *every* week and also there is always one invitation out and one invitation back and if we want to go to the theatre and/or cinema it's a fourth or fifth night; college functions have to be additional too. It's delightful in its own way – stimulating: over-stimulating in some respects – things seem to go at an hysterical pitch sometimes.

We had a marvellous supper with the Youngs. I was determined to be happy and jolly and everybody was – Brian still managing to come home angry and say, 'You're still in love with him' – but he didn't really mean it, he knew everything was alright; Nancy and I were friendlier than we have been in months. I needn't say what was underneath. I've never really fought so hard not to desire someone, I never fight against liking or loving people, but wanting to go to bed with them has to come into a different category, I am forced to agree. I still don't know if I'm going to make the grade: I stand a very good chance now Brian knows – but Frank doesn't help. Without wanting to or meaning to he makes things worse – intensifies things accidentally. Easily looks hurt or annoyed – over-reactive, which makes me so, which makes him so, which makes me so – and so on....

Sunday when I was in bed with my cold the Cromptons came round in the afternoon to ask if they could come and see the Wesker play in the evening on television – of course we said yes, if they didn't mind being given the flu – because my bed is always in the lounge nowadays so that Jane feels I'm still with her – not that you could keep her out anyway, but there's more for her to do in the lounge and a fire and so forth. (She's an absolute little so-and-so when I'm in bed, won't get off the bed or leave me alone for two seconds – I'm sure this is one of the reasons why we keep infecting each other.) Anyway I was looking forward to a restful evening – moan, moan – and instead of coming round only for the play they came early to make me some mulled wine. Wasn't that nice of them and what a bitch I am to be fed up with them. Angela was an excellent nurse: hot Burgundy (they bought it specially) with cinnamon, orange and other things I haven't discovered yet – it was absolutely marvellous of them. I am convinced that it was entirely Angela's idea, she looked busy and keen and he was completely uninterested. The drink was better than any other grog I have ever tasted: really superb; but they didn't go home until 12.30 even though I kept rudely burrowing down into bed and pulling the clothes up aggressively under my chin. So if anything the next day my cold was worse.

And that night the Youngs came to supper. I had to cook a dinner (she's done it twice to my *no* times). Frank was full of beans, chatty, teasey, bright. Ten minutes after arrival: 'You're behaving like a woman

with only one thing on her mind – serving the meal.' I
had to admit to having an awful cold and from then on
his mood was spoilt. I couldn't have checked my
coughs and sneezes for much longer anyway. He
made feignedly irritable remarks about catching it and
then said that it would give him the greatest
satisfaction to catch it. I pretended that this was
insulting because I saw Brian becoming progressively
uncomfortable – and then Nancy leapt at the chance of
interpreting it and said, 'Frank, you're always so nasty
to Margaret' – but she couldn't think why it was nasty
so I said that he would at last have a bloody good
reason for disliking me. He grinned. I felt I'd won, I'd
got over him completely, no feeling left for him at all.
Brian was my whole love and whole interest and I
hadn't got room for anything else. This is of course
true except for the hated bitch instinct that sticks to
me like a smell. Anyway as the evening wore on he
could see what had happened to me and grew
excessively weary and dark under the eyes and
couldn't sit up in his chair but slouched around until
Nancy was positively vindictive about him.

He came alive later and turned the subject on to
women, and how bloody it was to have to spend your
life repressing your lusts for other women (he'd had
some drink!) and what did we think of platonic
friendship (after Nancy had mentioned this) and both
he and I warmly denied the existence of such a state. I
was fairly honest – though decisively on the side of a
strict code of behaviour – and some of the honester
things I said seemed to hurt Brian, so I sat close to
him and devotedly held his hand and 'belonged' very
obviously and said that it was only my volatility

speaking – he knew that, it was perfectly obvious to everyone. Then Frank said, 'Cross my heart and tell a lie.' Nasty little debunking, separating jabs, cryptic insertions of this kind riddled my arguments. Whenever he said something like that little balloon-pricking remark, deliberately, with intent, I was momentarily at sea again, lost – the bastard! – I literally hid behind Brian's shoulder holding his hand and not looking at Frank. When I did so he was looking at me with questioning amusement and 'What good do you think that's going to do?' written in his face.

I wound up by saying that it didn't really matter how much we thought we wanted to go to bed with someone else, we never would and that was all that mattered. He looked really bloody after that. He got up and after spending about 12 minutes in the lav warmed himself in front of the fire. I asked him what was wrong, he said he felt excessively jaded. I couldn't help feeling full of affection and remorse. I was sitting right by where he was standing, so I very gently stroked his leg with my foot to comfort and say I was sorry. He brightened and said he felt better and sat down; and things seemed to pick up.

Just before they left he went to get their coats and my legs were sticking out in the way, and he said to move them because he wasn't a gentleman, he'd walk on them. I looked at his nasty expression and believed him and said so. When he came back he tried to catch my eye to show he hadn't meant it, I didn't want to see because I thought it would be better to leave things on those terms of mutual dislike. He said something provocative, and I pointed to him and screwed up my face to be rude but before I could get it out he grabbed my thumb that stuck out at right angles and held it close and said 'Gorgeous!' Everyone was silent and bewildered as to what interpretation to put on it. Still holding my thumb he turned to look at Brian and Nancy with mockery and defiance and 'it doesn't mean anything' all together in his expression. We all pretended to take no notice. But it opened me up again – wide, wide open. All I could think after he'd gone was, 'Why did he do it, for God's sake, when everything was finishing so well and neatly.'

For weeks before Christmas I refused to have any contact with him, in intangible ways put obstacles in his way at every turn – I was even beginning to hate him for giving me a problem – but underneath I was restless and peeved and vaguely irritable. Then he came round one evening to give us two tickets to the Christmas oratorio that he was singing with the cathedral singers. White, bleak, screwed up, fleshless, thin-lipped – tawdry, unloved-looking object that he was, he didn't stay as we had company and I gaily brushed him out of the door. He had been an overworked, irritable beast at home for a long while, according to Nancy. I came upstairs with the tickets, quite pleased that he'd spent 10 shillings on us. But without the slightest encouragement, in fact fighting like mad against it, I couldn't wait to see him there and hear him singing with the others and to speak to him afterwards.

At the cathedral he looked very pale and strained (not liking public ordeals of this kind) and didn't notice we were very near the front. His head darted about trying to find us. He only discovered us in the interval with an expression of relief and pleasure. Brian had been cold and went off to the parked car to get his overcoat. Frank took his place. Nancy was somewhere else in the audience, and we talked freely, excitedly, nervously, full of happiness for the whole ten minutes. It had nothing to do with me. It wasn't me sitting there alight with him. It didn't have anything to do with me, it just happened on its own, full steam ahead careering away with no let or hindrance, no mind – nothing. When we went back with them for a drink the same state of jubilation continued. It was as if we both recognised we had been fighting and had both given up simultaneously for a respite.

Early January 1964
In the new year they came to supper, and we drank a whole bottle of whisky – Frank, who drinks little, constantly asking for more. A sharp bout of aggression between the two men. Frank got upset over being given ginger in his whisky and honestly wanted to fight Brian over it – wrenching the bottle from his hand – he wanted the whisky neat – but Brian held on to it calmly, obstinately. I quickly interrupted. But foolishly Brian's been erratic this year: kissing all sorts of women he didn't really like under the mistletoe. He offered to kiss Nancy (and she'd have been delighted but at this stage was too afraid to risk reprisals). She pretended to be shy (after telling us what she'd been doing at a New Year's party!) but Frank wasn't going to be cheated: 'Let's show them the way, Margaret.'

First kisses should never be taken. It was so restrained as to be almost empty, but so meaningful as to be devastating. Without doing anything for seconds he held me so close to his thin body that I hadn't room to turn my head. I didn't think to turn it. My face pressed into his shoulder only. Then in some way I thought it was over and turned my face up towards his and his mouth was over mine before I could blink – very light pressure but open and soft and thin. We cuddled again afterwards – what a sight we must have looked. The restraint and sensuality of that kiss was unbelievable.

Such strength and masculinity! – but what am I going on about? I'm like a woman living two lives, a happy full domestic life and a sad, corrupt, ridiculous one.

I'm in a lethargic sick apathy about almost everything. What am I grieving about? – myself, I suppose, the impossible nature of my nature. It's depressing to find myself hamstrung at every turn. I can't go through another ordeal of the kind I had two years ago – on the other hand I don't know how to avoid it. I don't know any more what I want or don't want. I feel inexpressibly sad at doing anything to hurt Brian again. I'm sickened at my cheapness and shallowness, for though I mean with all my heart to refuse, I know it's on the books that I won't. I wish to God everything could resolve itself happily without trouble, just suddenly for everything to change, for the cloud to lift – for my whole nature to change or for something to cut across this soggy corrupt streak in me and seal it off from the rest so that my whole personality isn't contaminated and what's worse the life of my dearest man.

If only I knew why I ever get into this predicament! For some fiendish reason if a man who's attractive, intelligent, sensitive, with experience in common with my own makes a real set – I'm done for. I don't dream of setting up home with them – the thought appals me – but the innocence of the feeling I have for them and they for me seems its own justification, its own reason for being an accepted, a valid, a real and undeniably constructive experience.

If 'innocence' sounds phoney, let me explain. The men who put their hands on me too freely leave me cold, I can be amused and usually flattered but nothing more at all. But Frank doesn't intend anything consciously, he isn't too free-handed with an itchy paw – he doesn't ask for anything, he just gravitates, that's all. It's this 'gravitation,' preoccupation, and my knowledge of what he's thinking and feeling – he's so easily hurt, his face looks completely pained or happy, he's somehow given himself up – it's this that sets the trap. When he touches me it's as if he doesn't will it at all but as if his body betrayed him: it's the same with me. He can't help being one big question – unconsciously asking – unconsciously moving to you – what can you do but open your arms – you react unconsciously, like someone pressing a button, your arms open.

Late January 1964
I've had a disgusting tummy recently. Recently it has stepped itself up savagely and not only produced the usual constant running to the lavatory but also I've

felt really sick and constricted in the stomach all the time so that I can't eat. I've lost 7 lbs in weight over the last few weeks (which certainly won't hurt me) but I'd rather it were natural and not a sick process – I'd rather have some control over whether I eat or not – not feeling sick all the time. Anyway I'm getting better; I drink gallons of binding medicine and that helps considerably.

We went to see *Tom Jones* with Albert Finney as Tom. It was splendid, absolutely splendid. Thorough youthful high spirits – crude, fierce, robust: 'Let tomorrow do its worst, for I have *lived* today!' I'm fed up, I feel like kicking something, it's a good job the dog isn't in the room. Life is one bloody heap of restrictions after another. I feel I'm being paralysed by hair-fine but steel-strong cords binding me down like Gulliver in Lilliput. I shall go potty I think. That would be interesting, don't you think, yes, I'll have a little bit of pottitude for a few weeks, tear a few things up, run disgustingly amok! Isn't it marvellous the way spending a few days bashing your head against things can relieve the ache.

And I've been reading Durrell's *Justine*. The heroine interested me, self-concerned, neurotic bore though she is, though Durrell unimaginatively portrays her as the old-type *femme fatale;* her numerous love affairs are ridiculous and uninteresting and criminally unenlightening as regards her particular predicament as a person. He's concerned with setting the scene of a rotten world: 'This is what life is like, you know' – from Lawrence Durrell, who knows *all* about it! He yanks in any little episode, however causally unconnected with the story, that can

give you an ugly shock. He's really got a little peep
show of a world up his sleeve for you; and he's the
puppet master of ceremonies. What's worse, he's a
pedant and pompous and has mighty ambitions as a
'literary man' – he'll never use a simple meaningful
word where a complex meaningless one will do. But
in spite of all this, he has one or two interesting
aphorisms to make (spoilt by donnishness and over-
consciousness of the written word) and one or two
interesting scenes to offer.

February 1964
I've joined the Coventry Cathedral lay choir, the Saint
Michael's Singers. It's the choir Frank Young belongs
to – but he isn't the reason I'm going. He asked me to
join last September but I felt disinclined. A friend of
ours, Janet Whettam, a hearty, good-natured giant of a
woman, belongs to it and was very enthusiastic (as
Frank was). After I saw their Christmas performance I
was mighty impressed with the pace, energy,
intelligence of both choir and director. I mentioned to
Brian that I felt inclined to see if I could get in – Brian
was strongly 'anti' for 'Young' reasons. I accepted his
strong disinclination as guidance and left it at that.

However, when Janet came round with her husband
I said I'd seen them there at the cathedral and had
enjoyed the performance and she went off into
enthusiastic praise of the group. *Brian* mentioned that
I had thought of trying to join and instantly she
insisted that I must write right away as he had said at
Christmas that he was in need of a few more sopranos.
She wanted me to get out paper and pen at that
moment because the first rehearsal for the next session

was the following Tuesday and he wouldn't want to recruit after the session had started. I said I'd think about it. She was probably so enthusiastic because her husband's music was going to be sung – along with Haydn and Handel. Graham Whettam is a queer musical fish. Very short, very fat, *very* unattractive, rather opinionated and yet nervous, longish hair, velvet coats, etc etc – sweet enough. There is a rather poignant and fairly well-ordered romanticism in his music – he's one of Britain's 'modern composers' – gets quite a lot played.

To my surprise later Brian said he didn't mind if I joined, because he thought it sounded an exciting and interesting experience. I didn't write for two or three days – almost leaving it too late, then suddenly decided to. The director David Lepine must have got the letter on Friday – I had a reply on Saturday calling me to an audition on the following Tuesday at 6.30 pm and if I was successful to be prepared to rehearse the same evening.

He is an attractive, self-conscious, intensely emotional man given to quick, decisive opinions and making vastly differing impressions on people – some like him very much, some hate him. At the moment I fall into neither category. He was helpful and gallant to the nth degree when I first arrived but fiercely exacting when I was singing and sight-reading. I've never made such a public exhibition of nervousness in my life (I think I must have been undermined by my bad guts). I had prepared a song that I could sing with ease: and every time I went for the top note my stomach flapped against my breastbone and I screeched a good *two* notes higher than I aimed at. I did this mortifying trick three times – I thought he'd kick me out on the spot. But he persisted, changing the key several times and being very considerate. My paper literally flapped about so wildly in my hands that I had great difficulty in reading the notes. He didn't look at me for fear of intensifying my nerves – but I hardly think that would have been possible unless I'd passed out altogether (I was actually wetting my pants!). My sight-reading was pathetic, although as it was totally unaided I expect he took that into account, as he usually plays it through with the singer while he or she sings it. Anyway he said at the end that he was 'happy' and apologised and comforted me for my ordeal – and said how horribly cold-blooded it was: he was in fact a charming man but musically highly exacting. So there we are.

I loved the first rehearsal – the whole pace, energy, beauty of the thing: singing beautiful music with a lot of fine voices intelligently directed sent me over the moon. I couldn't sleep *at all* until 3.30 that morning.

I'd say that I'm the worst there by a hundred miles. It's a splendid group – marvellously stimulating – superb music to sing – I can't believe I'm in. I squeak away in the shadow of a magnificent soprano standing next to me. There are only about 15 in each group of voices.

It makes a world of difference to my mood and attitude if the weather's bright and clear and I feel that the world and life are limitless and tremendously evocative; and the sense of having so much to do and think and feel and the wonderfulness of it all sends me soaring.

March 1964

I'm fighting this Frank thing well – and think I'm winning – it's bloody sometimes but not so bad when there's lots to do – though we see far *too many* people for me when I'm as sick with colitis as I've been recently. It only makes that worse; because as soon as we see them the men start to tease and provoke, try to 'draw me out' as Brian puts it, so that when I sit back pale and miserable with the deliberate intention of being carried through the evening by the others I find within a few seconds that the tease and banter and sauce and charm that's sent across like ping-pong balls has got me engaged. And if I resist and hold out, there's always 'Why are you so quiet, are you fed up? – cross? – has anything happened?' etc. And everyone gets quiet because they think I'm sulking or something. Oh well, anyway when I'm fit it's great fun.

In some ways I thoroughly enjoy and really want and need an active social life – in others it's the last thing I want, instead I really need lots of peace and quiet evenings looking at telly or reading (not dull but somewhat passive). It's when I'm faced strongly with such a need that I find my timetable unbearable and there doesn't seem to be any stopping it. There are always three or four nights a week occupied of every week, but next week's timetable is typical of the sort of piling up that happens in addition sometimes: Saturday evening (they're all evenings) dinner with the Hanlons, Monday the play-reading club, Tuesday St Michael's Singers, Wednesday ballet at Stratford with the club, Thursday dinner with the Youngs, and then from Friday to Sunday our old Cambridge friend

Brian Murphy is staying with us. It starts off again the following Tuesday (with just Monday free) for another four nights: there doesn't seem to be relaxing space. I don't know how it happens. Sometimes I feel like shouting, 'Stop it, I want to get off!' – and sometimes I'm right in there spinning it.

April 1964
We've had a period of great turmoil with Jane recently. Not illness, bless her, but intense bouts of self-assertion and fight, fight, fight until I've become so exhausted that each day has seemed enclosed in a grey box and no-one can lift the lid. By a great effort we have all lifted the lid now, Brian and Jane and me. Now things are fine again – it's lovely. Things I knew would be different this summer term because the boy Jane used to play with in the afternoons started a full day at the nursery this term (Melanie has been doing a full day for nearly a year). Well, she started moaning and showing off for the first week because she had nothing to do in the afternoons: and she would do one jigsaw after another at great speed until she nearly screamed. I find it much more difficult to get her out in the afternoon now because I've given up my daily woman in order to help pay for my new bubble car – and I've got so many household jobs on hand I don't seem to have time to turn round. It's my own fault – I've really bitten off more than I can chew. Anyway things came to a head when she caught a bit of a cold and I thought I'd better put her to bed early to help her get over it. The sparks flew. She went to sleep at about 9.30 after two hours in bed, out of bed, screaming and shouting. For an *hour,* with excessive

and uncharacteristic patience, I kept going back to give her more kisses and more cuddles – it seems that she constantly wanted me to give her more love-ups – until I said that it was the very last time and I stuck to it. She rampaged interminably after this.

This then formed a habit and she did it the next night and the next and so on. I spoke to all sorts of people about it. I had already decided that it was insufficient occupation that was giving her all this steam she had to let off, and the stories I heard seemed to support this theory. Brian and I decided the only thing to do was to send her for a full day. She now stays on (with school dinners as well) and she meets her old pals. She says school dinners are much nicer than mine and she always has *two* helpings of afters. She is becoming a new girl again. She used to sit and make me push every morsel of food down her throat – and now she has two helpings! So I'm very happy again and she seems to be very happy again, although she is still excruciatingly disobedient but not aggressively so – I don't mind that, so long as her general aspect is one of a busy happy child, which it now seems to be. So there we are. Another domestic crisis successfully passed, I hope. Ain't life grand!

May 1964
We collected my bubble car. They've been all this time on the A.A. inspection and then doing what the A.A. man said and so on, and now after what seems an age of waiting it is home, sometimes sitting in the drive, sometimes in the garage. It's a dear, dear pretty pale blue thing and I love it. It seems that even with your foot flat on the floor you can't do more than 35

m.p.h. so that suits me fine. I have repainted the *inside*
entirely, all the metal framework and the plastic fabric
that lines the walls (pale blue and grey) – it looks very
beautiful – I get untold delight just looking at it. I
never knew a mere machine could give me so much
pleasure. I feel cosy and safe in it. I'm so pleased with
it, I found myself waking up the other night with the
image of a big broad blue nose in my mind – a bubble
nose; and I find a funny little patter going on at the
back of my head while I'm doing other things – it
goes on like background music: 'Bubbles: bubbles:
bubbles: bubbles: bubbles.'

Enough of this stupidity....

June 1964

I went to three rehearsals and the final performance of
the Mass last week and Brian says it's been like living
with a stranger. He says it was like my having an
'affair' with a piece of music. He's terribly glad it's
over and won't be starting again until October. He
said today, 'It's lovely to have you back!' – aren't men
funny! It has been very exciting and absorbing. Brian
says that the performance was very good indeed – but
then he's prejudiced. I think it was good though. The
general consensus of opinion that I was capable of
gathering in my dazed state after the performance was
that it was good. Perhaps we'll know more clearly
later. Today I feel like a limp rag. Isn't it funny how
absorbed one gets – to get so caught up when there are
about *sixty* of you doing it is very absurd – but an
awful lot of us seemed to be in the same nervous and
suspended state for about ten days before the
performance. And for a fortnight before this I'd been

waiting arduously for a late period – properly buggered up by it – as I am when my periods are late (they are usually so very frequent) – so no wonder that Brian feels like welcoming me back after a long absence.

We've been having the most disgusting weather this week – heavy, warm, enervating rain endlessly day and night. Before this – the hottest May I can remember. I feel now almost as if I'm writing under a rain-soaked, steaming bamboo-leafed roof – there should be jungle noises outside, there are in my head – I don't think I'm particularly well, perhaps that's why – both Brian and Jane have had nasty colds – I suppose I'm getting it.

July 1964

I'm so depressed. Jane has measles. She's been poorly off and on for about ten days now – temperatures, swollen glands, fiendish cough – and then a vast rash (not the measles rash itself but an incubating rash, apparently very common) and now an absolute caricature of a child with measles – she is *covered* with great red spots and large blotchy areas that look like birthmarks – spots even in her hair and on that scrap of skin on the perimeter of the ears and between her fingers; sore and runny eyes – temperature for days. I don't know how long the spots are going to last. I hope and pray Brian doesn't catch the measles from her – he's never had it, it makes me sick with worry – anyway, not to think about it.

Jenny keeps me wildly on the run – if I'm out of the room for one second it's 'Mummy – Mummy, Mummy, Mummy!' What else? – she's a very good

little girl with it really – very stoical – more stoical
than I should be, I know. 'Mummy, have you seen my
awful spotty face? – Look at my tummy,' and so on.
I'm developing a brisk efficient nursing technique so
as not to depress her. She responds well to it – makes
her feel she's not so poorly. Humorous, light-handed
and efficient, that's me. I crack up every so often but
it comes back again when I try. I wish to God Brian
had had it. Ever since I've known it was measles I've
kept him entirely away *all* day. I've not allowed him
home until the evening and then have cleaned the
house and disinfected all the furniture and myself
every evening before he comes home, and left all the
doors and windows open for an hour before his
arrival. My hands and face and arms are disintegrating
from washing and I change all my clothes each
evening.

September 1964
We have found an exciting and quite ardently
desirable pastime. We go country and square dancing
on Thursdays – and come back soaked with sweat and
annihilated with physical exhaustion. Such a
delightful form of exhaustion – the body singing in
every pore with integration and activity and leaving
you at one with everything.

It's for this reason I'm now a passionate cyclist. I
sold the bubble – that fretting, disintegrating,
mechanical product of a gadget-ridden mind – God, I
must have had a bad dose of the modern disease to
want the noisy bloody thing. I can't wait to get out on
the bike – I long for the times when I can legitimately
use it. My domestic timetable, such as it is, has been

completely chaotic since I've taken to riding into
college whenever I can – waiting in Brian's study,
perhaps going to lunch out with him.

The riding along the country lanes is more exciting
than the dancing. The only advantage the dancing has
is that I can do it with Brian. But the cycle provides a
keen solo pleasure. I love trying to ride up the hills
and perhaps finally having to walk – and then the
lovely free-wheeling – and all the time the one thing
that makes the whole experience marvellous, direct
contact with the air, the weather, the trees and fields
and cows there to be touched, smelt and breathed – no
bloody glass insulation everywhere you go. I adore
cycling – I adore pouring with sweat at the end of a
laborious journey (deliberately made so by the
keenness with which I do it) and being obliterated by
heat and exhaustion to the point of being unable to
speak. It's marvellous. I hum inside for hours
afterwards.

October 1964
Jane likes her new 'proper' school but is beginning to
grow dissatisfied. I'm dissatisfied anyway. These
teachers make you sick with their stupid indifference.
Jane has the strictest regimentarian in the whole
school. They do everything in single file. Jane tells me
it's rude to turn your head! All she says all day is
'Yes, Mrs Hawling; no, Mrs Hawling.' She was
smacked in the first week for fighting. She has now
been absorbed into the system and presumably acts
like a good little automaton, but still the system
permanently shows its deficiencies: 'Did you do any
plasticining today, Jane?' – 'No, I don't do

plasticining, I've got a reading book.' – 'Do other children do it?' – 'Yes.'

As regards the reading, this is even more unsatisfactory. She was given a book called Roy and Carol Book I. She instantly developed a mania to read, she wanted to read it to me, she said. I dutifully asked the teacher if I might read her book with her and was practically bawled out of the room by the surly bitch, who said in no uncertain terms that Jane did enough reading in class and she'd rather I didn't interfere. I was so humble in asking her in the first place, because I didn't want to annoy her; but I wasn't given a chance to explain that I only asked because Jane wanted me to. I acquiesced and came away and told Jane I couldn't. She was very quiet and surprised and then very depressed. After a couple of days I was convinced she really and truly wanted to read to me so I found from mothers what the book was called and bought her one. She read the thing in a week – I mean knowing all the words – and was looking for new things. During half term (a week) every single morning after breakfast she brought out some crumby old-fashioned reading book that a friend had given her (terribly laborious and artificial and about 40 pages long) and started to plough through it. She wouldn't let me out of the room to do the washing up till it was done. She'd work every morning for an hour and a half – and she'd be pale and tired at the end. I didn't encourage her – I did the opposite, I fooled around, tickled her, brought out crayons and started doing some – anything to distract her – but she'd only be distracted for about five minutes, then she'd say, in her own words, 'Come on, let's get on with it.' Or

she'd pick up a newspaper and start: 'This is a –
what's this word, Mummy?' I've never seen such a
fever to read. Every morning I'd find books under her
bed. She'd wake at about 6.30 and start chanting
away. So now, as I don't want to encroach on the
teacher's work, I've bought the first two books in a
different series for her to read whenever she feels she
must.

I asked Jane how she was reading at school. The
teacher never seems to listen to her, and then when
she did one day said it was good she was on page 13,
when in fact she can read the book from cover to
cover from pure memory, she knows it so well and is
bored with it. She is already beginning to mock the
chanting of words they do instead of reading.
Wouldn't any sane woman say, 'Alright, Jane, have a
look at Book II while I read a bit of it to you – then
you can look at it while I do something else' – or let
her look at a picture book or do some drawing, or
anything other than be stuck there with the same book
in front of her all the time. She'll get screaming bored,
she'll hate it – after liking it so much.

November 1964
Brian unfortunately has a violent allergy of some sort.
It has *covered* him in itchy spots. He finds it difficult
to sleep and of course it irritates all day as well. The
doctor has given him pills and sleeping tablets and
lotion – in other words, 'Just wait till it goes, old boy,
there's nothing I can do' – and all this aside we are
convinced it will be gone in a month – it was a fairly
sudden and violent eruption, which we feel will have a
similar exit. He has been overworking phenomenally.

I don't know how any one gorgeous, patient, determined human being can bear it but he does all his preparation and lectures. He takes a lot of sedatives, but we get phenomenally little sleep. If we have a good night we feel on top of the world the next day. He's also had a very persistent cough and this keeps him coughing all night too, so that what the spots don't do the cough does – but though he's so phenomenally active with his hands and his throat all night, he isn't all that aware of it the next morning because of the sleeping capsule.

We have had nothing but things going wrong this autumn. One becomes depressed and icy because there is nothing to do about it but sit on it, cope, hope it will soon be over and force a normality out of the life that remains.

Novelist and Critic

January 1965

It has snowed lightly for the last couple of days – but
it doesn't stay long and is a very dry snow, and with
the sun shining brilliantly all the time it is very
beautiful. I find myself thinking of Spring all the time.
I woke up this morning after having a dream of Spring
– of trees with leaves bursting open that were not
there the day before and of embryonic ferns sticking
out of the earth coiled and unopened but of such a
tender green and yellow colour out of the hard earth.

March 1965

Since I started writing my novel my life seems to be
changing. I require – in fact this is an understatement
– less and less in the way of social life. I'm constantly
asking Brian to change, postpone, if possible *cancel*
'doings' in the evening. I can't bear to have my
evenings broken in on. For one thing I seem to be
very tired – for another I want peace and close
harmony and can't be bothered by a demanding gang.
It is a kind of hibernation. We are in a position now
where people are likely to stop inviting us round so
often because we owe *five* different couples
invitations to us and have owed them all for weeks – I
can't bring myself to start it up. If I manage to get a

clear week except, say, for one night I'm terribly pleased with myself and feel I've achieved something.

This of course has its depressing obverse – I feel fed up often at the sedentary, internal life I lead, and crave to go out – but I mean walking, cycling and so on – warm, physical, active things – I suppose the weather will make this possible in a short time.

June 1965

An invitation we didn't want but couldn't refuse, to visit our old, somewhat estranged friends, Ian and Diana Train in Wakefield. I felt I had given myself in voluntary captivity for a few days – quite unable to think or feel like myself, with any honesty whatever – worst of all, unable to communicate with Brian, partly because we had hospitably given ourselves up, partly because we dared not talk for fear of being overheard in their much-crowded house.

We got there at about 2 o'clock on a Saturday. They had already eaten and we three had a salad on a table on our own while the whole Train family struggled noisily for assertion, one over the other, around the table. Ian went on talking through unheard-of clamour – Diana likewise. The three small Trains, worthy children of their parents, made insupportable assault upon our attention throughout the entire meal. Richard started up an endless chant as soon as we got through the door and before we sat down: 'We have *Winnie the Pooh* – shall I read you a story?' He sat on the couch for an hour shouting it. David, older and more sluggish, more impressionable to silent antipathy, just pulled out a police car with a first-rate siren and revved it endlessly on the edge of the carpet. Graham

– now walking – was up at the table shouting and clamouring for our food. The parents went on talking. My head rang with the clamour of wills and outraged egos.

Richard (who after all that, turned out not to be able to read *at all* – which is not surprising as he is only five) sat next to me in the park that afternoon still under the outrage of being ignored. He said, 'When are you going home?' I said, 'Tomorrow.' He said, 'Good, I shall be glad when you're gone.' I said, 'So shall I.' Later he said more to the same effect and I replied, 'Don't worry, I'm going as soon as I can.' David on the other hand, more responsive to one's attempts to be friendly, likes a tickle and a climb on Brian's back – and listened to Jane as if she's an oracle – and her sense of humour slayed him (or so it was when eventually they started to talk to each other, which was for about four hours on Sunday morning). He was very sad to see us go and said, 'I wish you could come every weekend.'

The time we enjoyed there, in an over-hearty way, was when we played charades. Diana and I fell into the pure acting of them with such gusto – even Brian with his bad throat *really* acted. We romped away – dressed up – did funny and horrible little scenes and enjoyed it in pure abstraction from the whole weekend. Diana is really a wonderful actress, very much better than me – I only give myself up to it, to the fun of it – she really acts and with real liveliness and spontaneity. In one scene Ian was a burglar – coming into the dark to tie Diana and myself up and only the street lights shone on his almost maniac face. I was genuinely terrified at the way he looked at me when he came in, and my quick breathing and gasps as he tied me up were half-genuine.

We had to be shown the glories of their home – not as their home, which one would respect, but as a social achievement. It was in the *best* side of Wakefield. Wasn't it beautifully situated? (there were some trees in the next-door neighbour's garden). The house is a good strong one – room enough really. 'Did the previous owner have children?' – 'Only the one' – with a look that classed them eternally as frustrated.

Ian was stimulated by his change of job to Education Officer and let me into the confidence that he is a very ambitious man and would really like to go into politics – although this last ambition, I think, is a secret. He also thinks he might have got a First at Cambridge if he had taken History for the second part of the Tripos and not Classics. He realises now he is in Administration (wry, fat smile) the great danger will be to become pompous. He must avoid the danger of becoming pompous.

I'm thrown into torment by the Trains. I would consign them to the devil gladly, if I did not feel that underneath it all they are lonely – in need of friends and support – like *all* human beings – and are in some way fond of us – I mean not simply as acquiescing springboards to their egos, but as people. I think I'll have to come to terms with my manic irritation with Ian by making a fair portrait of him in my novel.

October 1965
We went to our first social do in about six months – a party at the Cromptons. I got incredibly tight, I could neither see well nor walk well. It was because for

some reason I was exceedingly nervous – out of
practice socialising, I suppose. Brian had to guide me
about. I was very quiet and child-like, he says, so I
wasn't noticed much – also we stayed in a little room
where there were only ever six people at a time – I
wouldn't venture into the other room that was packed,
I was filled with panic.

When I was sitting in the back seat of a friend's car
with Brian, just about to be driven home, a kiss was
planted on my mouth from out of the night. I couldn't
see a face and no voice spoke – it was like a
benediction, in my maudlin state – as if the world
loved me. It was Matthew. I heard Brian telling him to
hop it but I never actually saw a face; shows you how
far gone I was. Matthew and I have been rather shy
and gentle with each other ever since – what a farce!

November 1965
Invited by our old friends the Beechams to listen to
the Birmingham Symphony Orchestra – it's the first
'live' concert we've heard in years.

We arrived in slight fog and bitter cold at about 5
o'clock. Claire opened the door and immediately
turned round and walked back to the kitchen saying,
'I'm feeding the baby' – we had to shut the door
ourselves and find our own way in. It turned out she
was furious with James for not being home yet – he
should have been home at 4.30 – so she really could
not spare a word for us when she was so busy feeding
Lia and cosseting her fury. We unpacked and I went
upstairs to make up Jane's bed. About ten minutes
later I heard James arrive – a polite, restrained male
voice, not wishing to engage in battle. Claire's voice

clamorous. She sent him out again to do some last-minute shopping.

I felt jaded, depressed, utterly fed up with the whole stinking set-up. James's 'I must not touch thee' role (after our brief affair four years ago) is exceedingly wearing, when it's not plain ludicrous – and yet he has to be near, and chat and see. He hates my being jaded and remote and indifferent – he's very gloomy under it and tries hard not to notice – but it is all I have left for him – why doesn't he simply go his own sweet way? Perhaps the poor lamb wants warmth and sweetness from me – in that case why wear such a martyred and resolute air? – 'I am a man who has suffered but knows now what is right.' This time he simply would not accept my distance – in spite of the row and nagging etc that had been going on since he came in. His face was alive with pleasure – 'It's wonderful to see you,' he said – 'to have you here' – and he kissed me in front of Brian and with Claire a few feet away in the kitchen. So I had a restless and morose Brian to cope with all evening – but James was full of happiness, quite impervious to everything. It is an astonishingly charming characteristic, this single-trackedness of his. He knows he's being a 'good boy' and so he feels fully at liberty to enjoy what is left to him and will not let anyone spoil it.

I'm trying to understand Claire – after all, she and James are the sources of the chief characters in my novel. To do so I must find out as much as I can about her – until now she has been a closed book. She has an Italian girl staying with them for two months – the child is ten. It was intended as an act of charity – holidays for poor children whose families had been almost put out of work by the flood in Florence a while back. Like most acts of charity on the part of women like Claire it arose out of a desire not to lose face. A Lady Bountiful friend, who also has three children, was in on this 'give holidays to the underprivileged' lark and she was having one. Claire felt she was being urged and wanted to look affluent and social-minded, and offered, and regretted it the next instant, as she admits – but hadn't the courage to back out. She has hated Anna ever since she arrived. Instead of the child being ragged, filthy and half-starved – lo and behold, surprise, surprise! – she turns up well-dressed and with a case *full* of clothes.

Claire said, 'Can you imagine my fury when I saw how much she'd got – four pairs of shoes! – much more clothing than my children – she's better off than my own kids.' I tried to explain to her that undoubtedly they had been planning and preparing for this trip for ages – probably borrowed clothes from friends and relatives – some of them look worn and rather large for the little girl. There was obviously a great deal of pride in sending their daughter to Britain – they certainly wouldn't want to appear poverty-stricken. Claire didn't seem to get the idea.

The child can't understand a word of English – or so Claire says. She also says she has learnt nothing since she's been here, and calls her stupid and lazy in front of her. I think she is wrong – I think Anna understands a *lot* – she is morose and silent because she is terrified of Claire whose eyes blaze at her. Every word Claire speaks to her is delivered like a challenge or rapped out in contempt. She is mean with food to her – I can't understand the woman. When I said how agonisingly lonely she must be away from her family, unable to communicate easily and how frightened she is of everything, she said 'No she isn't – she doesn't feel a thing.'

Well, what can one do? She has lovely black eyes. Fortunately she is strong, a sort of leathery endurance about her – she can manage it all – she won't become hysterical or ill as far as I can see. But I should think she's not likely to forget her English experience in a hurry. James protects her and gives her little cuddles – almost furtively. He talks to her – has learnt some Italian words to be able to, and speaks them very well – smiles at her a lot and calls her 'good girl' – lifts her up and so on. Does his best, but it is all in the teeth of Claire's opposition. He was actually reduced to saying in front of us, 'I think you're mean to Anna' and Claire said, 'I thought she was meant to be treated as one of the family, not something special.' Anna never says a word, nor laughs, nor sings – nothing. You just see her black hair and eyes, sallow skin, gold earrings – implacable.

December 1965

I am unfortunately going through a spell of bad tummies. Blasted people, I think – wear me out in the evenings and then I start work frayed in the mornings. In any case I'm letting up for a few days in order to get less tired. The lids of my eyes look like zeppelins – full of water – standing out like fish in a white lake.

Also we now have been forced back into the old play-reading group once a fortnight where I have to suffer and respond to Matthew's ridiculous crush since the kiss after his party. He gets a flood of hormone every time I enter the room and is as modest as a schoolgirl. I can't help but respond superficially – I'm made that way. I feel flattered, warmed – made more radiant, affectionate – with me it's like pressing a button, I've long been amazed at it myself. I refuse to bother with it – it is all completely unimportant to me – but I resent the tiredness it produces when I want to be quiet and utterly uneventful, in order to do what I find I am passionately interested in doing. I cannot abandon the idea of writing for the rest of my life – it becomes more important and more inseparable from my life every day. And yet I haven't that enormous quantity of physical strength that is required to manage everything well – so I keep falling foul of my health and having to spend a few embittered days (or even weeks) resting up.

I've nearly finished the first draft of my book. When it's over I'll pause a bit and then revise it – it's very much a first novel and will need so much done to its frail carcase. Beginnings are always unsatisfactory but one has to begin and put up with it. Perhaps by the time I get to the third or fourth novel I shall feel I am in some measure expressing what I want to say. The very technique at the moment commands almost all my attention – like a child learning to walk, I can't quite use the skill yet for the purpose of getting from one place to another; and I get tired quickly, it is such an exacting job. I'm so looking forward to when I can stroll and run and cover great distances.

I both resent and envy Matthew's more easy-going attitude to literature, both reading and writing it. I see his attitude as self-indulgent – but that's how he sees mine.

I said to him recently, 'Where do you look for a keener, more complex understanding, if not in literature? How do you help yourself if not by sharing experience with others more alive, more honest – able to put you in touch?'

'What an appalling thought!' he replied. 'Do you think we're all spiritual cripples? I don't want putting into touch, thank you. I don't look for clues to my soul's salvation in literature.'

So much the worse for you! I thought.

April 1966

We seem to be pulling out of our unfathomable slough of winter ill-health. It has been disgusting – the last term, nothing but ill-health. Now, we have had a week of good weather and we have been out in it as much as has been possible, and we feel better – we feel like people again rather than animated corpses. How wonderful it is to feel fit and able to cope with things – more than that, to be able to more than cope with them – to find that you have energy to spare.

To bring this about, I haven't been writing for about two months. About six weeks of that time was taken up almost entirely with family illness – but nevertheless not writing in itself is a rest-cure. I've decided I shall not write *at all* until the autumn and I shall fight tooth and nail to keep Brian off his research work. We are going to live physically active lives for the next few months to give us back some life-energy – we are becoming washed out nervous wrecks, physically as strong as a sheet of paper – which I'm sure our skin grows to resemble more every day. So 'new ideals' for the Buckleys for the summer season:

more and more physical activity in every way – sun
and fresh air. Brian has bought me a bike so we can
go cycling together. We have been doing this for the
last few days and it's marvellously refreshing. God,
am I glad to see the back of my book for a season – in
spite of the continuous temptation to take the
wretched thing out and go through it, or worse still,
start a new one. It's a running battle, and will be for a
time, but I'm determined to spit at it – as I do
essentially – scorn the whole bloody business. The
obsessional undercurrent is there all the time – but it's
not going to finish me off!

May 1966
I'm at Brian's college again – that's nearly every day
this week, mostly by bike. I fancy I'm beginning to be
regarded as a harmless eccentric by the odd folk that
meet me here nowadays. I must say I feel a bit of a
damned fool – particularly when I'm hauling an
electric fire and alarm clock into Brian's study and am
intercepted by students and cleaners. Students are
almost as used to seeing me here as Brian. I don't
know why I come in so much. Normally it's for the
exercise on bike – this being my 'keep fit' season. But
apart from that, Brian likes to have me here – partly, I
think, to protect me from going on some binge at
home – gardening or house-decorating (both of which
bugs are biting hard since I've sworn off the novel for
a season). I don't know why I must be always on
some binge or other, but so it is. Once I have decided
to let up on something the pressure must be eased by
something else, so there is always something to be
done vigorously following hard upon the heels of

something else. I have at the moment a mouth full of ulcers and a troublesome chest – so perhaps this is why Brian keeps whipping me off to the college.

November 1966

Last month we went to a party given by Professor Hunter, who is head of the new university English department. He's a funny, highly strung, nervous chap – highly sociable – about late forties, I should think. Always looks as if he's on the rack in company; glassy-eyed with the effort to be intelligent and entertaining as well as sociable. I'm in a very fortunate position as a postgraduate's wife – no real connection with the university – I can be as simple-minded and as coy as I like; and I like to be both of these. I much prefer watching at this stage; and as I'm very much younger than most of them, this is taken as a sign of respect. Hunter is always pleased to fill up my glass and entertain me – flirtatious in a most donnish way. Part of the time full to the brim with sophisticated back-chat and innuendo – next minute drops on all fours to pretend to look for a peanut I've dropped – making no attempt to look for it but having a good squint at my ankles. Then I am circulated to an impossible group of 65-year-olds.

Now, having been to so many of Hunter's dos and being some of the last to invite him back, we decided to do him the honours. It was an agonising prospect and an agonising evening. What made it really terrifying was that we invited Miss Joan Browne (Principal of the college) – an invitation five years overdue. She was the one I was most frightened of having home socially. She's a famous old bird – head of the largest training college in England, administers with superb calm and efficiency (to be not much disparaged by 120 staff you must be pretty good). She is also a big wig in all sorts of other spheres, local and national – a *very* awe-inspiring old bird. Both she and the professor are nearly 15 years older than us which puts a very natural barrier up against easy conversation in the first place. Add to that the fact that we felt we could not talk freely about either the college or the university and you can imagine we felt as if we were trying to balance on one leg all evening.

But I achieved the greatest culinary success of my life that evening. Mushroom soup, followed by steak cooked in half a bottle of red wine with mushrooms, bacon, onions and thyme – and roast potatoes and celery braised in sherry and butter. Followed by a concoction in which egg yolks were whipped into a jelly which was later frothed up and moulded and decorated with fruit and ginger.

Miss Browne tucked into all courses like a navvy – Prof. Hunter and his wife more abstemiously as becomes those surfeited with the aesthetic pleasures – aesthetic because I swear that meal extended beyond the realms of gastronomic delight. I was overjoyed because I am a very erratic, frequently very poor cook – and literally *anything* could have happened that night – particularly as I had been in a state of screaming high-tension for a week beforehand and on the day behaved like a demented thing. As far as one could ever say that such an evening was a success, that one was – so I expect one must be satisfied. The older generation talked about plays they'd seen before we were literate, we were patronised – and agonised –

a loathsome business but one that must be gone through – fortunately, once in a blue moon.

Now we must try, after Jane's half term and such distracting events, to get back to a regular routine. It is a great wonder, I often feel, that I ever write anything, the way my time is cut about with domestic events and ill-health – but it's wonderful – I would live no other way.

April 1967

On the whole it was rough staying with my parents in Cornwall this Easter. Mum seemed tight, irritable – damned glad to see the back of us – with all the to-ing and fro-ing of feelings that come with this. One minute punishing us for being there and wearing her out further – next minute making ferocious claims, implying ingratitude, indifference and so on. Unable to face the fact that she was too tired and I was too tired. I've asked them to come at Whitsun as usual but I hope they don't – I could do with a few months gap from them this time. Perhaps she'll recover more quickly as Spring goes on. Being at their place is one long battle to deny one's life. No responses, no living, except in the statutory allowance in between coffee, shopping, snooze, TV etc. Above all no self. I think they would truly hate the person I am – it is so foreign to them. My development has been arrested at fifteen for them and I conform unconsciously – very keen to please, and hating it to illness. I try to arrest the changeover in me but it's always imperceptible – I'm there before I'm aware of it. Well, it happens to everyone.

I said to Mum, 'I've written a letter every week this term – been good, haven't I?' 'So you should,' she says. I let it ride. I try further explanation: 'But when I've been writing my novel in the mornings it's all I can do to look at a pen again afterwards – I want to turn my back on it.' She wanted to say something but thought better of it – I read it though: 'No-one makes you – your duty to me comes before anything else.' I have an almost uncontrollable urge to tell her where she stands – to go on about my first duty being to my own life – but how can you? She is poor, weak – made a mess of her life in so many ways. But I *will not let* her cling.

June 1967

I see in my father vigour and infirmity, a little immediacy – no, a lot as regards Jane and a little as regards me – and a great dead sea of automatic response. Jane doesn't disturb him too much – a kitten, delightful, growing. With me he draws out the few threads he is familiar with, that he can make a contented pattern with. For the rest I disturb him – only his peace, for he knows that all is well between us.

I felt very tender towards my parents this visit (opposite to the last when my mother and I fought). This time she was confiding and close. Told me much of her life with Dad and me as a child that I did not know before. Claimed me as a champion. I tended to defend her against Dad – it pleased her and did not much disturb my father – he saw we were striking up a temporary bond. Once or twice though he seemed put on a spot – he is old, his assurance shaky. I feel great natural sympathy for my father – for my mother generally it has to be worked at. I'm making her a vast cardigan. She told me she never had the heart to throw away the only jumper I ever made her (twelve years ago) and would I knit her something else. I'm working like a demon on it. I can't forgive myself for this piece of obtuseness – why is one always so much more obtuse towards one's parents? Can't afford the sympathy – too busy defending your territory – like war.

July 1967
We took Jane to see a film about a lioness, called *Born Free.* Terribly sentimental – I grizzled all through it. Jane thought it was great. We also took her to see the Ballet Rambert – load of half-bakes – average physical age 18, average mental age six. It was a matinee when OAP's get in for a nominal sum. They spoke to each other in deafening *sotto voce:* 'My gawd – 'appy, ain't it!'– this on the prolonged dying activities of the White Clown of Innocence. God knows it was stupid and pretentious enough but the audience was worse. Poor old geezers – poor young geezers. I dislike ballet. One should dance in rhythmical, fluid, flesh-weighted movements – all this straining after bodilessness makes you sick. Stuck up on a stage too – they should be in an arena, where you can join in if you feel like it.

Anyway, Jane liked it – along with the ice-cream in one interval, orange juice in the next and ice lolly in the third. All part of a little girl's treat. She is beautiful. Jane is more understanding of people than any little girl I know. She is too good to me sometimes – and Brian is too, of course – but Jane is just a child. I feel entirely undeserving of the understanding I receive from them – I don't know how ever to give enough back.

October 1967

The Flemings, whom we've known for several years, from being the shyest and most retiring of couples, have turned into avid seekers after intellectual conversations and play-readings with us, tireless performers of Greek and Elizabethan plays. I was always a sucker for this kind of thing, and Euripides in particular *is* fascinating: those primal passions – love in *Hippolytus,* sensuality in *The Bachhae* – impossible to control or even understand, murderous if thwarted but regenerative if expressed. But now with my writing to do I sometimes resent the effort. The only thing is, Natasha and Barry are so genuinely interested in finding out and exchanging experience and working out their salvations one way or another.

Natasha is a bluestocking in appearance – a rather heavy jaw and small clear eyes, the face confidently exposed by the fair hair being drawn back and upwards into a firm ridge that runs along the top of her head. Conversation with her is interesting enough to draw me regularly on my bike across town to where they live. She sometimes takes me by surprise with a pointed observation. Once when I was complaining to her about my lifelong disability, lack of confidence, she remarked, 'To my mind, Margaret, you lack confidence about as much as an anaconda!' Brian laughed a lot at this and explained that people generally noticed in me not the anxieties themselves but the vehemence with which I over-rode them and the articulateness I used to do it.

Barry is one of those tutors who wish to be recognised by their colleagues as burdened with work and conscience. He joins in the general partiality at the college for investing coffee and lunchtime gossip with an air of suffering, exhaustion and baffled earnestness. They all need to gain assurance of worthiness and usefulness, and regularly whip their ideas into a froth – the words *creative, self-expression* and *maturity of understanding* are favourites and hallowed. Whenever I enter Barry's study at college I am taken aback by shelves and shelves of books on all sides and floor to ceiling. Responding to the density of the books, the smell of the paper and soiled bindings, the sound-absorbent effect of their mass, I feel a kind of panic – it's the sudden assault of quiet oppressiveness, with, at the nucleus, a soft-spoken, well-dressed, solicitous man whose compactness is as suggestive of unlimited reserves of remote information as the books themselves.

Spring 1968
Mark Turnell is a newcomer to the college English department. He is writing an enormous six-part 'experimental' novel about the affairs of a family – like *Buddenbrooks* or the Forsyte Saga – called *The Explorers* – divided into sections, one called Waitings, in which all the waitings occur, and so on.

I have seen him at the college going to a seminar, in nervous anticipation evolving the light birdlike but enthusiastic manner that he regularly adopts. It requires a certain dramatic performance before a large group to bring his kind of lecture off well. It seems to him logical to assume that if you are stuck out in front there it is your duty to entertain as well as inform and elicit thoughtful response. What's needed is a felicitous combination of sociable enthusiasms for most literature – dogmatic obstinacy against some that gives his personal taste definition – and a generally picturesque and charming presentation of the lot.

I've had glimpses through a half open door of the performance itself. He removes his cigarette with a prolonged and thoughtful gesture of the fingers at the lips. His thin delicately shaped lips are smiling, as if the smile were suspended waiting for an object. He flicks his blond wavy hair from his eyes with an impatient gesture. As the strain of the lecture increases (and the need to keep the ideas fluid and indefinite) so his smoking grows faster and more urgent. He puts out one cigarette and lights another, his brown-stained forefinger and thumb held tensely away from him as if they were alight.

In the front row I noticed his two favourite girl students who attended with every fibre of them but didn't listen. It stimulated and comforted him. He drew on them for confidence. When he quoted, if the quotation could be lent any intimacy of tone or delivered with a brash extravagance, then he delivered the lines to them and stole from the words and from the liberty of his delivery some extra nuance to his relationship with them. Occasionally he gave the words an innuendo they were in fact innocent of. He was playing a double game, partly to enhance the excitement of feeling between himself and the girls and partly to keep at bay his anxieties as to the

soundness of his lecture. With the girls it worked –
they were willing – but the men fidgeted.

Spring 1969
We invited a couple to coffee and drinks, a research
student from the university and her recently married
husband (she 27, he 36). He lectures at the university.
Pale, greying, academic, very shy – calls it
'observation' – says he prefers not to take part – very
repressed – blushes at almost any kind of response.
She is a bird-like predator upon other people's
experience, carrying the field of logical enquiry into
the living world. I first noticed her at one of Hunter's
parties as a dauntless little figure – the distinct, rather
strident tones of her voice raised above the level of the
other conversations in fierce intellectual dispute with
her tutor, who looked exceedingly hot and pale with
an unhealthy flush on his cheeks. She has become less
strident since she married. I think she will turn into a
human being – I think her husband might – although
he almost left it too late. We have seen them a few
times before. He says, after a few formal preliminaries
like passing round infinitely meagre salt biscuits with
an atom of cheese on them, and a glass of sherry –
slowly, with a cultured American accent to Brian: 'I
think it is time we talked about *Women in Love*.' We
hold a sort of Socratic dialogue. Then Belinda after a
pause, to me: 'Say about Life!'

They're all right, really – I can see I might become
quite fond of them, and dimly foresee an opportunity
to involve Belinda in my portrait of Winifred in my
novel – I need a 'control' over the self-portrayal. But I
often dread seeing some of the other university people

– and I often feel I need the loose sangfroid and merriness produced by too much wine to see me through it.

I lie awake at night sometimes, hating those self-locked, self-concerned rattling nonentities. The misery they produce in themselves and in others! The endless, exhausting, totally unrewarding task of selling themselves to others. The only property worth having is 'intelligence' (I'm beginning to loath the word). If you are one of them you horde it – keep it under lock and key – try to dazzle acquaintances with what *might* lie therein if you were so unsophisticated as to let them see. You panic at challenge; shy from sensibility; and hate the man who has committed himself to anything, however small – if he has shown himself to be concerned, to have a passionate interest in life, he must be a fool.

I want just a very few, a *very very* few friends with whom one can talk and feel an inter-communication and understand further by their talk without having to take into account that they are mostly rather mean, rather frightened, rather selfish, rather stupid, rather warm-hearted. Just *a few* honest and intelligent friends. Not this silly pony-trot; it tires me out. We're very bad at returning invitations. I say: 'We've got a whole week of free time – hang on to it for dear life!' But we *must* have them back because in spite of it all they *are* looking for friendship, are in need of it, *want* to be liked.

March 1970
My novel is completed and sent off.

And now a second honeymoon for us – life gets more and more full and wonderful. I've always enjoyed sex, but I was deeply upset eight years ago when a doctor told me that if after so many years of marriage I wasn't achieving orgasm, it was unlikely I ever would. Now, when my gynaecologist asks me if I regularly have 'a good orgasm,' he's bowled over when I reply, 'Yes, five or six' – and he starts taking notes! But it's been the hardest job I've ever had to do, to overcome the barrier set up in my long intimacy with my father. I felt like Odysseus fighting Proteus: as soon as I got a good grip on the problem, it escaped by changing shape into something else. I don't think I'd have won through without the extra assurance given me by writing as well as I have and winning Brian's admiration for it.

The victory has been so important because to me life energy is almost indistinguishable from sexual energy, and sexuality the one open circuit to our lives – the one obvious physical dependence on other lives: the one thing that breaks us out of the personal shell, the personal struggle for survival. And orgasms are all-important because they're the agents of release and connectedness – without them you're missing out on the finalisation, like being amused but never laughing.

It is crucial especially for a woman because her sexual hunger is so much greater than a man's – it makes us such slaves in expectation and such demons in disappointment. Sexuality suppressed promoted all my exaggerated fantasies. How can any woman have a hope of equilibrium without regular sexual satisfaction?

April 1970

Now I've settled the shaky objectivity of *A Woman's Man,* I am curious to see how Flaubert dealt with the same problem. After all, he said, *'Madame Bovary, c'est moi.'* Winifred was me too, at first.

Flaubert wanted to use his heroine as a vehicle for some of his own feelings. I know to my cost how turning a main character in a novel into a mouthpiece or representative puts a novelist in a tricky position. It poses problems of integration and balance. The need to express the experience of life that is closest to you can usurp the function of the main character. The complex necessities imposed by the fact that it is a novel and not simply a piece of sensuous satirical writing are then given secondary importance. The temptation is to correct this imbalance by superficial stylistic tricks, such as mockery or satire of those very sentiments to which you have already given exaggerated attention.

That's what Flaubert did. At each step in the story Emma's neurotic condition is placed in a context that heightens the justification for her withdrawal into an intense dream world. By the pettiness, meanness and stupidity of the life she leads and the people she lives with, as Flaubert conceives it, her self-involvement and withdrawal are to be partially exonerated. In this way Flaubert caused the obsessions he identified with – those of a disappointed idealist or dreamer – to be lifted on to a nobler plane than mere sickness.

May 1970

I went to a lecture at the university by F.W. Bateson called 'The Novel's Original Sin.' I was tense and excited. There were aspects of my time at university that I had greatly enjoyed, and these memories were now awakened. I felt the elation I had sometimes felt then before a lecture when I admired the speaker. I'd not read any of Bateson's work, so I permitted myself this excitement – he might be a surprise, might have something to say that I could think about.

A stout bald man rose, his face flushed and shiny. He surveyed his small, intimate audience. His round eyes appeared to gather confidence and pleasure from the survey. I recognised it as a professional gesture – a moment's calm, an apparent establishment of contact with audience before he began. He cleared his throat.

'I've decided to put the cat among the pigeons properly today.' His voice, high and gleeful at the start, had reached a sonorous, drawn-out low by the time he got to the last words. I was prepared to be amused. 'I propose to delineate the ultimate hideous nature of the novel – to contend that it is an inferior art form – and I propose to do this to an audience composed, no doubt, of novel addicts to a man, and especially to a woman.'

Somebody snorted with appreciative laughter – thrown out like a rose to a primadonna – and there followed a more general hum of repressed, self-conscious appreciation. I was both irritated and amused. I looked around me. Clearly he knew how to touch the raw nerve of self-esteem in his audience. They looked stung, but how could one object to anything so playful – and wouldn't one make oneself look rather foolish if one tried?

He went on: 'The novel can never achieve the beauty of form achievable in a play or poem. It is too long to be memorable, and as history it is inaccurate. If a literary genre is neither reliably informative nor capable of close relativity, let us give it the *coup de grace.*' A wide and chimp-like grin was given us at this point, displayed from one side to the other before it was withdrawn. 'I simply cannot condone serious novel-writing or reading.'

He could not continue for a moment because the audience could not control its taut-wire hum of laughter. He was patient.

'Is it history?' he continued. 'No, it doesn't claim to be – but it is pseudo-history, presented as unverifiable fact. It is untrue, masquerading as true.' He lowered his voice to a menace. 'The most we can say for it is that it has inter-subjective possibilities – but so does an exchange of daydreams. A novel is a daydream confused with real life, a limited subjective process pretending to reality – fiction posing as fact.'

He poked fun at the realism of the typical nineteenth-century novel. Then, pausing to give a grateful grin to the more persistent gigglers, he exonerated satiric narrative from his criticism – 'and the nearer we move to allegory the less danger there is of confusion with fact' – and embarked on more predictable areas of literary criticism, with knowing references to some of the novels of Forster, George Eliot, James and Lawrence.

Long before this I'd had enough. My amusement at his technique had died. I looked down at the table in front of me, put my handbag on it and started fiddling with the strap. As he struggled to outrage or invert, to squeeze out the last dram of laugh potential, I became more and more depressed, and then disgusted – and not just at him. I bent the strap of my handbag backwards and forwards, backwards and forwards with such fierce pressure that the plastic cracked. The sight of it encouraged me to crack it more – to make patterns of cracks along the breadth of it.

What a miserable situation! It reminded me of something else – what was it? It was the audience participation that reminded me. A long time ago, at Brighton, when it was raining and we had nothing to do, Brian and I had gone to a wrestling match out of curiosity – we had never seen one before. And for a while I was completely absorbed by the sight of the heavy sweating bodies with rolls of flesh around the waist – the slapping and thumping of them on the canvas – and driven almost hysterical at the cries and groans of pain the wrestlers gave out. For explanation I turned to the audience and saw that they were alight – bright eyes, fierce gestures. The wrestlers were playing upon their nervous awareness of the possibility of real pain and physical suffering. People stood up, shouting, 'Kill him…. Twist his ears off!' and booed when they didn't act well. I couldn't forgive either party.

Here it was arrogant laughter that was being called for. How did they all get caught up in the game of putting the authors down? Was it to feel themselves as good as them in understanding life – or better, since they had more discrimination? I couldn't work out exactly how poor Bateson had got himself into this mental corner. It bothers him so much that novel facts aren't real facts, that a novel is the result of one person's vision. Couldn't he see that poetry, drama and philosophy were also the products of one person's vision? – more abstract and therefore more dangerous and delusory.

When the audience started asking questions I felt better. One young man attacked the criterion of memorability. 'Does it matter that you can't recite a novel?' he said. The sound of earnest honesty in his voice was like a gush of water over paving stones.

A tall and bony woman, whom I recognised as Germaine Greer – we'd met her at one of Hunter's parties – supported Bateson's preference for symbolism over realism by referring to the 'mimesis' she'd seen among Australian aborigines (they were pretending to be aeroplanes) as 'a kind of cultural disenfranchisement.'

Bateson nodded and sipped water. A reply came from a young postgraduate, who stood up and flicked back a long strand of hair as she turned first to him and then to Germaine: 'Why do symbols have to be so obvious? Good so-called realism is full of the most subtle and complex symbols. The characters in a novel, for example, are people-symbols. If you feel that the purer the symbol the better, then you might think one of the highest forms to be the gesture of the first two fingers of the right hand.'

I snorted with laughter for the first time, then looked round furtively, anxious that my only betrayal of a sense of humour should have been of that kind.

Bateson was conspicuously studying his watch, and now the chairman wound up the meeting. The audience scraped back their chairs to talk to each other, completely ignoring the Professor's exit.

Spring 1971

Enjoying Brian's sabbatical year – constantly in his company. I've always chuntered – my name for the endless verbal work-out or work-through I do, going over events, impressions, thoughts, problems – starting at one end of my mental intestine and coming out the other. I used to do part of it in letters to my friend Mary, but gradually I've found I can do it best with Brian – and he's found he prefers it to any other form of interchange. Sometimes he just uses me – I don't mind – a bit like Pozzo with Lucky in *Waiting for Godot,* who says, 'Think, pig!' and Lucky is happy to do so because that's what he's made for, it's what he's best at. Brian reads out something and asks me what I think of it and I cough up.

Like Lucky I often go on too long – when Brian wants to get on with something else – and sometimes I follow him out of the room – into the loo if necessary – to finish what I want to say. He pokes gentle fun at me. Once at a restaurant in Oxford he spotted a Max Beerbohm caricature, *Coleridge at Table,* with Coleridge spouting while all the others are fast asleep with their heads in their pudding bowls, and he burst out laughing: 'That's you!' But in his bossy, protective way he's taking over more and more of the practical world of housekeeping, and though I'm grateful to be rid of the anxieties I associate with it, I do at times complain that his treatment of me comes close to that of Swinburne after his breakdown – 'Time for your walk, Algy' and so on.

Summer 1971

Some of our neighbours have got into my College novel. There's Mrs Cullum, the egomaniac next door, irritating everyone within earshot, whose lawn has now been mown so obsessively that it looks in patches, particularly in hot weather, bald. Her flowerbeds are all pebbles, no blades of grass or weeds, and in winter when only the dormant bulks of one or two perennials remain they look like pits for the condemned.

Then there is the middle-aged married bachelor at number 22, who got into the novel through a scene which burnt itself into my memory. One day he told Jane off for walking on his front grass, and I lost my temper:

'What do you think I'm going to do,' I said, 'tie her up? You're not going to make my child's life a misery. If you had children of your own you wouldn't be so damned fussy.'

We were both frightened and sweating at the ordeal, both reduced to inarticulateness within a few moments, each making the other worse, screwing up every ounce of courage to sustain the attack – my bowels in knots, his lined face screwed into distortion and pale with the impact of my fury. He turned abruptly and walked tensely away. His neatly tailored sports jacket and well-pressed trousers looked independent of his nervous body – unruffled by the chaos they contained. His hands clenched, his thin shoulders stiffened, his walk looked mechanical.

The Harriots opposite are more congenial. Their daughter Pat is newly-divorced from her husband and living at home again. The young pair seem to want to talk to us a lot about their problems – not together of course. Pat watches Kevin turn up to our house and flounces back horrified, then later feels she must come along and put her tale of woe:

'Whenever we have a row, he's always sure it's my fault, because of my colitis, and when it's over he forgives *me* because I'm ill. It's never *his* fault – it couldn't be, you see, because he's well and well people are all saints, it's only the poor irritable sick who've never any right on their side.'

Neither of them want to discuss anything – they have no intention of making an effort – they are both as blind as bats, made thoroughly insensitive by what they feel to be their own grievances against each other, and want merely to justify themselves to some third party and gain some sort of public acquiescence to their decision.

Kevin is prone to unconscious attempts at suicide – he nearly killed himself and the infant Alice when we were taking a swim with them in the college pool, by carrying her into the deep end although he couldn't swim (Brian raced to them, threw Alice to me and dragged Kevin out). He invites us out a lot. We find excuses not to go. Mean? – no, there's nothing we can do – there's a limit to the number of times you can comfort someone. I soon reach the point where I want to attack – to say, 'Do something about your situation, you slob! – move! – get your wife back or get someone else. Move!' Anyway, their trouble all seems to stem from the idea of the holiness of the self – *I* have been hurt, *I* have been unjustly treated, *I* am not loved enough. Never imagining that the amount of love or understanding *they* ever gave, you could put in a thimble. But they are people. You can't tell them this, you have to comfort. But there's a limit!

Jane has taken Alice under her wing. It is misery watching the three-year-old's pathetic dependence. She sometimes wakes up in the middle of the night screaming for Jane, who represents security somehow. Sane patience and understanding and affection – endless patience and generosity towards all her waywardness and whims – is what Jane gives her. Jane seems to have bags to spare and generally attracts poor lame ducks to her.

She is a strange person that, allowing for the usual maternal disrespect in the matters of everyday living, I have a very great deal of respect for, in as much as she remains an unknown quantity to me. She has been completely unruffled by not passing the 11+ exam and has a gigantic good humour and indifference to those who strive in this respect. I say gigantic on purpose because it does not strike me as indifference dictated by ineptitude but is in fact endowed with enormous good will towards the strivers. Coming out from school she has the mobile face of a clown and the stumbling, rather shambling walk expressive of her greater height than the others (she's tall for her age). Her bright eyes look good-humouredly and friendly towards the dogged but are always on the lookout for a laugh or a send-up of teachers and all seriousness.

1974
Writing our commissioned book on the novels of this century, it's the minor writers who are the stumbling block. Their aims seem journalistic – a mulling over of the known – a desire to form and reform stale or

undeveloping thoughts in ingenious plots that are meant to do their thinking for them. Each turn of the plot or each stance adopted is intended to pose a point, but they are always heading away from the people or situation explored. This is because so many of their responses to the real are deadened by their urge towards the fake. Permitted concepts and allowable directives leave no time for the joys and dangers of real exploration. Society at its most obvious – its limited and limiting products – is always under the microscope, never individuals – they are too complex and burst open theories, threaten the manageable. Old directives are exploded, the current ones obeyed.

Golding turns upside down the classic boyish ideal of innate nobility and innocence in *Lord of the Flies*, and then in *The Inheritors* swallows whole the equally daft notion of the innocence of primitive man. Powell in his *Music of Time* sequence, instead of exploring the dynamics of growth pats on the back his diffident young shopper among makeshifts for the future as he turns into a dubious old collector of relics from the past.

I see I'm intolerant – they are sensitive and responsive – but when I read them, as I have to for parts of this book, I feel as if I'm inside a jacket two sizes too small – I can hardly breathe or move and end up wanting to rip it off.

April 1978
Walking around Corfe Castle at night, taking notes for my novel *The Commune* which is set in this area.

The streetlamps light up the mist – it forms a lightish glow behind the castle and hills. Going down a dark lane – very narrow, very steep sided, with overhanging trees. Very cold and windy in spite of the mist. The cottages look as if you could step into their bedrooms from the street. Signs creak in the wind. Streets peter out to where there are no lights at all – even at the centre where it's well lit, you look down a side road to see complete blackness, like a black curtain drawn across. If you don't confine yourself in this lighted area you get a sense of being completely lost. If you go down one of the lanes where there's this deceptive whitish light being reflected from other sources, it becomes mysterious and unconnected with your usual experience – your sense of proportion disappears – dimensions are all out. Unreasoning fears. The texture of the air is very wet and very cold. Extremely strong presence of the hills at night.

Yesterday in the open countryside I was thrilled by the shadows of cloud passing over the sweeps of hill. So much blustering fresh wind – walking in it made me unable to talk, unable much to feel anything about my two companions – just responding to what was going on – to the walk, the wind, the hot, the chilliness. It locked me up – at the same time releasing me physically.

I'll use these scenic details in the book. When I began it I had no idea it would bulk so large. It's taken me over gradually, irresistibly, like a phase of life. Now I'm midway it feels as though all my life is being funnelled into this great digestive system. This is what I've been wanting all along, what I've been preparing for, a fast interplay of many different styles of responsiveness. I've always felt I had no set personality – that I was fluidly reactive, capable of many lives, and I would live out my potentialities in my novels. A friend of mine once said, 'What can you do if you have two conflicting needs?' He's lucky to have only two – what if it's 102? – you have to be always shifting your ground to accommodate them. He complained that you can't alter your nature, but I'm always doing it – or bringing other aspects into play by shifting the grounds that activate them. There's nothing fixed or limited in our so-called nature – we all have 90% of our potential we never use.

When I heard E.M. Forster's remark, 'If you can pretend you can get inside one character, why not pretend it about all the characters?' I thought, *That's what I'm doing!* I need the liveliness – passion and stimulus from all sides, an excited sense of expectancy, of endless potential in the given situation – that comes from so many different responses to it from different characters. I want to shift an intense inward focus from person to person in a chain – like a barn dance, link-break-link – and not just the personal emotions but the general thinking, that too individualised yet linked. All this is working to underline their aloneness and their togetherness, the one made meaningful by the other: which is one of the book's themes.

All my life I've felt a disturbing energy in me that's like a separate force or being, something that has to be released or expressed. It makes me ready to do or say anything for a bit of fun or excitement, making me appear a fool or a child. All that potential would have turned destructive or self-destructive if it hadn't found a creative outlet. I no longer feel – not every day, at any rate – ready to stamp or shriek like a child who can't stand the boredom of going on at the average adult's pace. One or two hours of writing this book each day uses up some of this energy – with luck, enough to give me a semblance of normality.

Death Threat

May 1980
An hour after we'd been given the bad news about
cancer in the breast, I looked out of the window to see
Brian walking miserably round the little park outside
the hospital– and when he spotted me and I shrugged,
guess what I was thinking? Mad as it sounds, I was
taking on the prospect of death as an adventure – the
extreme opposite to Beckett's view of living as dying!
But what I most strongly felt was what I said
immediately to the surgeon advising mastectomy: 'I
can't die – I've got too much to do with my life!'

In the ward there's endless hysterical fun – half
plain terror, trying to keep all the events that must
happen to them at bay and mentally at arm's length –
terribly touching, making me feel tearful often – but at
other times impossibly annoying, like being in a
birdhouse that has just heard the fox has been shot –
squawk, giggle, soppy chatter, exaggerated, not to say
tall stories, all going hell-for-leather, all at once and
all so terribly high-pitched, as if everyone's voice has
gone up an octave. The atmosphere is naturally
intensely friendly – everyone of us needs with all our
hearts to get on well with each other, to listen to each
other, no matter what we say. I seem to say far less
than ever in my life, but I listen and nod and throw in

the odd loving word with great gusto and completely genuinely (perhaps not quite completely all the time, but often, that's an accurate description) – the facts of the situation for us all make it inevitable.

I can see the fear and the sense of 'unbearability' in the faces of the patients and it seems instantly to me that I can help handle it for them, by which means of course I'm handling it for myself – going out towards people full pelt is another way of escaping oneself. I'm also a very co-operative and undemanding patient – what on earth else is there to be? All these things are leading towards one's final freedom – how can you possibly put obstacles in the way?

October 1980

Dad's visit. We said we still loved each other though we couldn't stand living with each other – and we both felt better. But my hospital experience has altered my feelings about his ageing (he's eighty now). I find the signs in him of approaching death very hard to handle. I'm at my wit's end half the time, with thoughts of insanity and suicide. Sitting with him, listening to him wheezing helplessly like a sick child, I burst into tears. The child in me loves the remembered father – hates this impostor. I explain some of the difficulty to him and he smiles as if he understands, but several minutes later he's shuffling about as before, humming his four lost notes of a forgotten tune.

I'm incessantly washing my hands, and have to explain to Brian, 'My anxiety about dying or growing old is like an electrical charge, it's got to go somewhere – I discharge it down the plughole!'

Yesterday when Brian came out of the study, which Dad uses as a bedroom, I asked him where he'd been sitting.

'On the bed.'

'Why didn't you lie as usual, you sod! You know how I feel about that sort of thing. He sits on that in his dressing-gown and at his place he puts that on Grandma's bedcover, which hasn't been washed since her death. So now you'll have to have your trousers cleaned! I feel shattered. I can't get rest at any time, while he sleeps continually. His decrepitude saps my strength!'

'You treat him like a leper – you won't let him touch or even breathe on any food but his own – why don't you check your revulsion as I do, by boosting compassion?'

'Yours is mild enough to be repressed, mine isn't. It's the same with all our feelings.'

'He's seen you put your hands over your ears when he coughs and shut your eyes when he swallows.'

'Shut up! – you're tormenting me – I'm wracked with guilt already.'

The middle of the week at last. Jane has come home from university unexpectedly for the night, explaining to me, 'I wanted to come home midweek because I miss you, but I want to go back to go to the carnival with Clive, to get to know him more.'

'But you know I've been longing to see you this weekend, after Grandad goes. You'll skip other weekends, I know – and I can't go on suffering like this in expectation and disappointment. I need the close, developing intimacy with you, and if you put

that at risk all I can do in self-defence is cut back –
then you can come home or not as you wish, I shan't
care!'

We were shouting at each other in the kitchen, and
Dad listening in the lounge called out through the
hatch, 'You'll only put her off, talking like that!'

'As if I'd be affected by that – I'm not cringing!' I
said, and slammed the hatch door.

Jane and I went on quarrelling, then she left the
house to walk in the dark alone. I joined her and we
talked for another hour.

'I need Clive and the sexual connection,' she
concluded, 'but I'll try to be more balanced, to
socialise less and work more.' Then, in tears, flinging
her arms round my neck: 'I'll always love you more
than anyone else!'

At bedtime I went to Dad's room to make it up with
him. For a moment I responded to him as a person, not
a symbol – and there he was in my arms gasping with
gratitude like a man in a desert who finds a well. Why
do people suffer so in isolation? I find life so intensely
difficult.

After his departure, watching his washed bed sheets
on the line, I felt such a conflict – pity and horror.
What drives me insane are the conflicts I can't
reconcile – that there is no reconciling. I feel people
can't get into touch with each other – that it's an
illusion. Perhaps I should go away and be on my own.
I have an almost uncontrollable urge to disinfect again
every object in the house.

I cried, watching Brian under my instructions
putting Dad's sheets in the incinerator. I said, 'His
winding sheets. I can't forgive him for dying.'

'You identify with the process.'

'But I didn't in hospital.'

'There you were in the front line – all feelings switched off except those needed for immediate survival. Now they surface – related to Grandad.'

Listening to Mahler. It helps me: the music is how I feel, constantly – the complex death stress I want to deal with, wash away. That second symphony: I just can't get enough of it. The energy, the restless alertness to every menace – the clashing, thumping affirmation set against sliding, unbalancing doubts – earthquake tremors of dread and mistrust! And at the end of the first symphony, how the menacing or sinister is woven into the resolution as it moves towards the final triumphant positive – the shuddering persists in the background but woven in, making the ending valid. The ending of my novel will be like that.

But there are days when I run from one anxiety to another. Have I touched my blouse near the missing breast, after accidentally touching the skirt that's taboo? (I've forgotten why – somehow connected with hospital or Grandad or Grandma or disease). It burns me, I must take it off! On these days I feel sane only when working or watching telly. Brian says he's worried about my growing obsessionalism: 'Twenty minutes to wash up what would take me five – an hour for weeding a patch five feet square – half an hour to make up your face because you have to wash your hands between every separate task.' Yet it's the same sort of anxiousness that drives me to get my work right. It seems that as my writing intensifies my whole imaginative world does, the neurotic alongside the creative. And how I miss that fiction world of mine if I stay out of it in the everyday world, even for a couple of days. I can't live, can't breathe properly without my normal rhythms of talking and writing.

December 1980

Shaffer's *Amadeus* at the National Theatre. I thought it corny and vulgar. He can't portray Mozart as a human being, only as part freak, part god – a clown with divine gifts, a dwarf with a jewel in his ear. But what crashed through the Shaffer barrier was Mozart's own responsiveness, open to any impression or impulse. People only need to be more like him, with that energy, urgency and confidence, to enjoy the same creative freedom.

Alfred Einstein in his biography says that Mozart, 'by the very fact of his towering genius was unsuited for this life' and had 'an inability to behave sensibly and realistically.' They're all in a conspiracy to make genius look inhuman, at the same time as trying to cut it down to their size. They find that the clairvoyance and the gusto have a disconcerting force, so they see the one as arrogant, the other as loony.

Einstein said Mozart's wife 'did not deserve his love because she was not fitted to share his thoughts.' Another mean academic presumption. They shared what was more important to him, a warm, unreserved human intimacy – as well as a satisfying sexual life: didn't he write to her, 'My little fellow is longing to possess your sweetest cunt.'

February 1981

Watching a TV programme which demonstrated that human protein is only nine amino acids different from a cabbage (out of a total of 150) I said to Brian, 'So I feel again the continuum of life: Hallo, cabbage, I eat you because we belong together.'

'And the cabbage replies, That's okay, my lot will get round to you in the end!'

'Ugh – you cynic!'

But the mystery of non-human life fascinates me. Don't plants have a kind of intelligence, inorganic substances a kind of life? Death may take us across the boundaries. Even into slime moulds – I can see them as an attractive after-death destination. To imagine my individual unity – this fortuitous and unnecessary complexity – scattered among millions of smaller consciousnesses makes death seem a possible adventure. And looking at the crystals in the Natural History Museum I felt how wonderful it was to belong there too! – half way in the continuum of organic and inorganic.

When a friend dismissed the 'physical and chemical' in favour of the 'transcendent,' I said, 'But don't you see it's there, in the physical and chemical, and not in our limited spiritual understanding, lies the only source of change and renewal?' Whenever I read about the latest quantum theories, I feel the same: this is a table because we register it as such. A photon passes right through it – the idea makes me feel totally associative. Einstein needed the security of a God who 'does not play dice.' To someone like me, who's always known on the pulse how dicey life is, the notion that the whole universe is the same is no shock at all. God is dead but so is death!

One of Jane's boyfriends called my attitude to death 'the most reductionist I've ever heard.'

'No,' I replied, 'it's the most expansionist! Imagine us dissolved into our constituent elements to become part of other forms, organic and inorganic, with their own forms of consciousness.'

'But I want my own to continue.'

'Forever? – how appalling!'

What egoism there is in the kind of search you find in Tolstoy's *Confessions* for a relationship with 'the infinite' – a fixed contract between him and a knowable eternity. He was always looking for a moral hideout. I need the thought of endless adventure, nothing fixed – my own personal mixed with the endless impersonal. I see the finite as infinite – infinitely changing, infinitely unknowable and on that account infinitely surprising, refreshing, entertaining – as well as sometimes a nasty shock.

June 1981

Walking on the Burton Dasset hills with a new friend, Ingrid Kent. She revealed that her marriage is virtually at an end – 'I don't want to heal it,' she said – but I pleaded with her not give up:

'Part of your trouble is your own jammed defence mechanism.'

'I admit I'm damaged, but I can't help myself.'

'Yes you can – if you talk out all your feelings with him, including the resentment and guilt.'

'I can't – when he criticises me I just shut down, or cry and leave the room.'

She repeats to me the factors of her situation as she sees them, stuck in them as in a wheel The only way to break out is to set in motion the mechanism of affectionate response deliberately, as an act of faith – faith in the outcome. There's so much envy, jealousy and spite between them – animal responses that she sums up in the one word 'incompatibility' – so transferring them into a world of fixed abstractions that nobody can do anything about.

At times we're like sisters – I share all her feelings – but next day I boot her around in my head for making me live like her. When I'm with her life seems so desperately piecemeal – such a fluttery preoccupation with this brush stroke or that leaf formation. And I have to push aside my sensitivity to her need – her loneliness, her clamour for affection and interest. I'm so susceptible to that kind of appeal – and I have to hide, be secretive about activities she might want to share, otherwise she'd climb on my back.

She made things worse in her marriage by adapting herself dutifully to the role her husband Victor had been trained to allot her – it took years for her revolt to gather force. Few men can feel passionate love for a mirror – or not for long. That's what Ingrid instinctively does to a man – poised to take on his response. She's always measuring up to roles, with anyone. She said to me, 'You make my ideas whirl' – and that's just what happens: it's like a pin-ball machine, I say something that pushes her out of a fixed position, she whirs around and drops into another slot.

Being with her I'm learning a lot about handling Sheila in my novel.

October 1981

Victor Kent and Jane have become lovers. I'm half
crazed with guilt at the further strain on a marriage I
want to save – and half amazed at my ability to ignore
it all and go on with my novel, my need to write is so
great.

Victor, coming to collect Jane for the evening, stood
in the doorway, kissed my hand and then my lips,
gazing hungrily at me. 'It's all screwed up, isn't it?'
he said. 'If you can't save us, nobody can.'

He does want to be 'saved' – shown how to live – I
can see it in his eyes, alongside the sexual. He finds in
Jane, as he put it once to her, 'something of your
mum' – and she jumped on the statement at the time:
'There's nothing of Mum in me!' He warms himself at
her physical and mental wholesomeness and learns
from the Buckley-talk watered down to a level nearer
his absorption rate. Of course he revels too in the
crude juvenile funfulness made romantic by sex – a
perfect escape for both of them. But he's always
askance for something else. Two months ago he was
attracted to me. He still is. I feel as if he's getting to
me through her – having her instead of me. If Jane
knew this she'd go berserk – and yet part of Victor's
attraction for her lay in wresting him from me! What
an awful burden I am to her – it's as if in trying to
prepare her to cope extra well with the world I've
equipped her with three legs – so that she's constantly
falling over one of them! If I've released her from
conventional inhibitions, it's only to impose this
worse one, of my influence. She needs to rebel against

it, follow the flow of her own feelings, yet so many of those are dictated in reaction to me, and besides, she desperately needs my blanket approval for whatever she does. Very well, I give it.

I feel overloaded with people yet intensely isolated. I need to slow down. These past weeks I'm constantly flooded with emotion and my brain has to work overtime keeping topside up. I feel like a runner going faster and faster – a race of articulation – to gain the prize of some measure of peace, of temporary understanding of the flux of chaos. Why is it people like me malfunction in the world where everybody else does well enough, and excel in the world where the others hardly function at all?

Though I'm exhausted I'm writing well. In these scenes of love and conflict at the end of my novel everything seems to come together, fast and inevitable. I've been obsessed with suffering recently. I see life as a struggle, full of conflict and pain. What I write in this chapter I see around me and in my own experience.

December 1981
Evening with the Rushbrookes, who served some strawberry wine and talked of their plans for joining with another family and settling on a small 'self-sufficient' holding in Wales or Cornwall – doing in fact what in my novel I projected for the characters based on them! Their thirteen-year-old son has warned his mother that Dad's main motive is to spend more time with the other woman. Tessa told me she did recognise 'the possibility of losing Adam' but was committed to the project 'on ideological grounds.'

Adam said he wanted more physical work, and the 'isolation' appealed to him.

Brian, seeing how close all this is to what's in the novel, afterwards accused me of 'sorcery and witchcraft – you read his palm!'

'I just read his face,' I said. 'The tensions were all there.'

He's got thinner, and is less strikingly handsome, but when he comes up close to you and looks you in the eyes and goes Boom-boom! he's still a knockout. I've never known anyone do it more effectively – make a woman go weak at the knees – and the more effectively because, I think, not deliberately. He knows the effect he's having of course – he does it to everyone and has a whole troupe of females waiting for him to do it to them again, but he doesn't know how just he does it, doesn't calculate, exploit and savour it. His sexual demand is actually reinforced by his denial of it.

I believe he's made a bargain with Tessa, conscious or not, to be available at her customary practical level while he forages abroad for spiritual food. It was that self-inflicted imprisonment, together with an equally strong urge to kick over the traces and break out, that caught my interest at the start of *The Commune*.

February 1982
A bowel infection activated my colitis, lasting several days with intense pain and a fainting fit in the middle of the night. Having Brian with me while I shat – touching and supporting me, with my head pushed up under his sweater and pressed against his belly – allowed me to relax enough to avoid a faint. With him

there I floated into a semi-consciousness, in which I couldn't focus my vision or control my limbs. Afterwards in bed I was so exhausted that even the movement of a finger caused gripes. I lay suspended, waiting, avoiding his face because it looked so alarmed.

To be without him in these circumstances is unthinkable. He makes it bearable. I live off his effortless loving.

Recently he complained of the pain he felt watching my tenderness towards a close friend: 'You gaze at him so radiantly sometimes.'

'That's because he's the only person I can really communicate with, apart from you and Jane. Anyway, I do love him – I've got to have someone else, someone different to love. You are a fountain, he is a stream. And I want that other family as an extension of my own.'

'Think of it the other way round – wouldn't you feel hurt?'

'I couldn't stand it, I'm much too insecure. If he went away I'd get over it but without you I couldn't live. To me you're not a person but a force of nature. I don't love you – I live you. Anyway, I'd trample him into the ground in any close association – he's not strong like you and Jane – you both have such a cut-out system, you can switch off from me and follow your own pursuits – and come back at me too!'

My openness with other people, even Jane, depends on the feeling I have in my soul of exclusive possession of Brian. I'd be a different person – more cagey, even a hermit – without that security. One day last December when the two of them went out together leaving me for three hours on my own, I washed up obsessively for about an hour, then wrapped a shoebox in pretty paper and filled it with picture postcards – another hour. I was so tense – my muscle pains were intense, my throat ached – I thought I was going mad. For a while I sang Christmas carols out loud. I thought I'd have to hit the booze – if they'd been any later they'd have found me plastered!

'I missed you so badly,' I told Brian. 'You've no need to worry about my affection for anyone else. Affection is the product of plenty. In your absence there's none for anyone else.'

April 1982

I've been talking a lot with Jane's new boyfriend, Paul Brown. I was relieved to find I could play conversational ping-pong with him as easily as I'd been able to horse-play with her previous one, Andy Gibson. I was grateful to him and pleased to find a young mind so agile. Then I began to suspect he has a tick-tack mind. He pecks about the surface of things picking up all sorts of unrelated facts, so that when you mention a topic – Pop! – out comes a fact – and he's so pleased!

I share with him a constant need to be entertained – I can't bear to be locked in one set of responses. I also sympathise with his need to stay clear and unpossessed, keeping responses free and guarded from pressures. He's got a stronger hold over Jane than her other boys because she can't 'put him down' mentally – he wins arguments simply by shifting his ground before she can get him.

For a while the non-stop conversation was an escape bubble for me. Then I got irritated by his high-pitched giggle, the grating monotone of his voice, and a soul so practical it makes me feel lost. Andy Gibson was so unformed you could imagine a lot of growth potential in him, but in this one I can see the whole length and breadth and not-much-depth, and I feel he can only add more of the same – and he's got too much of that already! I was interested for a while in his rationality but now I feel constricted by its lack of scope. He's always on his toes looking for the obvious.

I said to Jane, 'Why do you offer yourself as a dumbbell for him to flex his ego?' and to Brian added, 'Why is she drawn to him?'

'Perhaps she's trying to get unBuckleyed – independent.'

'What's the use of being independent and wrong? Can't we all share the same rich ground, roots intertwined? She should go for the open-faced, open-minded, generous souls.'

June 1982
Victor Kent calls in occasionally for a 'consultation,' bringing out scraps of paper where he's jotted down the things he wants to say about his problems with Ingrid.

At the end of their party a few weeks ago he picked me up (he's a big six-footer) and charged round with me slung over his shoulder. Ingrid's two friends ('unmarried but living together') went pale with alarm. He's so sensual, he badly needs physical contact – who doesn't? – there should be more of it – but everyone's afraid of the sleeping sexual dragon.

Once as he drove away from our house I called out to him, 'You're loved!' and said to Brian, 'I could go to bed with him just to comfort him.'

Last week before he arrived I was wondering whether I'd have the energy to do the passional identification that gives him what he calls a shot in the arm – I might have to eke it out with touching and cuddling. I felt like one of those harassed and bedraggled hen birds with a chick bigger than herself fluffing its feathers at her. To have this great thing towering over you wherever you turn, demanding you should cough up everything – it makes you want to run away and hide. And I feel guilty whenever this kind of thing happens with friends because their need of me makes them award me 'love' – the highest credit anyone can give – and I don't feel the same because I don't need them in the same way.

He was worrying about his depressions and obsessions.

'I know,' I said, 'that it all goes back to your childhood, with an unloving and dominating mother, and I don't know what you can do about that, but the symptoms at the moment you can deal with. It's a mixture of hurt, resentment, longing, nostalgia and guilt, isn't it?'

'That's it!'

'You can break out of it, with other people – especially kids – by going along with them down their trail of interest, grateful for their selfish preoccupations. It's what I do all the time whenever I'm with people – as well as in front of the box! – and there's nothing more refreshing. I know all about

obsession. I'd do anything not to be shut up in myself
– locked up with a lunatic!'

'What you say is absolutely right for me – you
won't leave, will you? You're able to enlarge a whole
aspect of my vision – like blowing up a photo – so I
can study it and get it into focus.'

After a long talk he and I were laughing and joking
like kids, on the couch watching telly – and he went
home refreshed.

Today when he arrived it was hot and we went out
into the garden. He picked me up, held my bum over
the sprinkler, chased me with it and finally held it to
his chest. Both soaked, we changed into towels. He
flashed his genitals and threatened to whip my towel
off. Laughter and shrieking – except from Brian, who
was decidedly constrained! For the rest of the evening
Victor sat on the floor in the gathering twilight talking
about his sex life. At the end, while we were drinking
coffee and listening to Handel's Water Music, he said,
'There's nothing like the Buckles for putting a fellow
in touch with himself. I feel I could go out now and
dance in the fields!'

July 1982
Summer holiday with Grandad, whose altered face,
after his recent operation to remove a tumour near his
chin, was a shock: deathly pale, with a three-inch scar
alongside and under the left ear, his mouth pulled
down and unusable on that side, and the bottom left
eyelid hanging out and reddened. He was pitiably
shrunken, and shuffled around, the heels of his
slippers banging on the floor. But his character and
spirit were unchanged. In the evening he dressed up to

watch television with us in a monkey suit acquired in a sale of a dead man's clothes. In that, his ashen complexion, twisted mouth and dark glasses suggested a gangster or croupier in an old movie.

I was desperately fighting revulsion. I hate my Howard Hughes complex. Everyone I know has more contact with everyday reality than I. Brian pleaded with me not to think about death, but I saw everything in terms of it – the holiday-makers pretending happiness – what a futile farce – why carry on? Everyone I looked at I loathed. In rejecting death in my father I found myself rejecting the life that leads to it. And I hate Brian's composure – what is it but indifference brought about by suppressing his rejective impulses? I'm like the dreamer of a nightmare who can't wake up but can only escape from it into another painful nightmare. The 'not thinking' Brian advocates is impossible for me.

Dad has told me how reassuring touch is. I see his daily woman Averill sitting on his lap cuddling him and I feel guilty. I don't like to touch him, let alone kiss him – it's like embracing my own death. I dread taking him on a trip in the car – it's like carrying around my own coffin!

He tottered about Truro, his hanging eyelid watering.

'I'm blind and deaf and daft and completely useless!' he said in the restaurant while I was in tears across the table, hiding them behind the menu. Determined to disregard his infirmities and provide an enjoyable experience for us, he ordered a mixed grill he couldn't cope with and sat watching us eat our steak and fondues. With some friends in the evening he was asleep most of the time but gamely provided a limerick about 'a young woman from Tottenham' for the tape we were compiling.

'I hate your being old,' I told him, and he replied, 'What do you think I feel about it? – I don't want to die.'

Just when I'm overwhelmed with so much pity and love I think it must break all the barriers between us, my stomach flaps in physical revulsion and I can hardly bring myself to be normally human. When will I be able to take him in my arms? I feel I've got to perform an impossible task, like walking on water – yet everybody else can do it easily.

On the last day I admitted part of this to him, burst into tears and embraced him.

We left, calling out 'See you soon!'

Brian said he replied quietly: 'I hope so.' I didn't hear.

It was the last we saw of him.

September 1982
Violence between the Kents. Why does she provoke his anger by dismissive coldness – she knows it will – and then leave the room, go to bed and 'dread his footstep'? In that cry, 'Kill me! Kill me!' when he burst into her bedroom there was manic defiance: *Do your worst, I defy you!* Does she trust him to hold back from really harmful violence but want to bring on a crisis that would justify demanding his departure? She desperately wants to justify herself – to prove to others and herself that her actions are right, that she's the injured party, and so deny her half of the responsibility.

I told Victor, 'You're a barbarian! – you've no more sympathetic understanding of her than a child. Is your professional social work no more than a cover-up for this? She needs time to explore the potentialities inhibited by her life with you, and you need time for your own emotional development. Gradually you might come together – but not if you bully and batter her.'

When he came round for his 'Buckley fix' he was obsessed with his 'white-hot anger' with Ingrid. He kept returning to it, as if he were laying out a pack of cards for me to interpret. At first I was too tired to give him what he needed, that is, himself explained to himself in terms that might promote the positive. I felt I had to describe the aggression in such a way as to rob it of its guilt and glamour, but at the same time help him see his egoism as a legitimate need or power source which couldn't realise its demands unless it took other people sympathetically into account. He's like a dangerous polar bear who has to be warned he must behave or he won't get his fish.

When he'd calmed down he wondered why he and Ingrid had never talked about their difficulties together.

'Too busy playing roles,' I said – 'and if things went wrong, well, life was like that, to be endured – hence your suicidal feelings. You were ashamed of your responses and at the same time proud of what produced them.'

October 1982
Jane has come home after the collapse of her effort to live with Paul in Nottingham.

I said, 'You thought you were cutting the apron strings and found you were tying a noose.'

She looked ill and lay curled up or sprawled out, silent, grim, unresponsive, pained – as if she were rejecting us as well as him.

It has taken three years of distress to get me to the point of accepting and even at times preferring our daily life without her. Now we go into reverse. She and I both fall back on to roles that neither of us want any more. We'll have to create new ones.

I saw her this morning sitting on the loo with her head hung down to her knees, the picture of abject depression. So I did my midwife job on her and an hour later she was on her way out, all smiles, ready for her day. I know I shall be all given up to her problems for a long while – but I have to go totally with whatever situation I find myself in. I've found that if you withdraw from one set of tensions you saddle yourself with another set created by the withdrawal. There's no other relationship like the mother-child one – nobody who hasn't experienced it would credit how overriding it can be.

January 1983

My father's funeral. At the sight of the coffin I couldn't breathe or swallow. I went through the ceremony in a daze, not taking in any thing except the presence of the coffin – feeling, *What did he want to do that for?* – and irritation at Averill blubbering behind me.

At the reception several sherries carried me through conversations in which I gave away all his possessions except two antique pieces of furniture and the photos.

People were struck with wonder and gratitude at what was governed by neurotic fear and rejection. I only wanted to keep those things that reminded me of him in his prime when we were so close. Looking at the photos, I find my parents, especially my father, so beautiful when they were younger. My relationship with my him was erotic underneath – no doubt about it – my tummy turns over when I see photos of him in his thirties and forties – hence the violence of my rejection of his old age.

After a day at home Brian and I made love. As I was about to come I saw a vision of the coffin. Suppressing the vision inhibited orgasm, so I let it stay. Denial and acceptance in one.

July 1985
Wengen, Switzerland. I feel disoriented. All I see up here is death. The mountains are brutal, massive, frozen. For me the only beauty is in the welter and incredible variety of the flowers – life under stress. My feelings are as frozen as the scenery. Where's the elation and excitement I expected and normally feel anywhere? At a recital this evening the pianist excused himself from playing a Chopin piece. He couldn't do it justice, he said, because the altitude didn't agree with him. Perhaps that accounts for how I feel. I lack the oxygen I need to be myself, to have the pace and passion normal to me. I feel slightly sick all the time.

Yesterday, high up in the Jungfraujoch I envied Brian's grinning radiance – he called it 'the elation of imagined supremacy' – after he'd stood at the edge of the observation platform looking out over the frozen landscape. When he led me there I felt nothing – frozen with terror. He tried to get me to see the high peaks as symbols of both death and achievement: 'Confronting the one leads to a sense of the other.' But I get enough of that kind of confrontation in everyday life. If I wanted a representation of elemental life-powers on a grand scale I'd go to the jungle – my eyes are always on stalks whenever I see it on the screen – but I just couldn't stand it physically. Anyway, you don't have to travel – life anywhere is a jungle.

September 1983
I've written the last chapter of my novel. In Mark, my main character, the suppressors have reached into every corner, until death is the one great freedom. Bess, whom he's loved, is now a convenience in his passage to death. Death is the only way of association, of belonging. That is the conclusion I've moved him to.

Mark balancing in the wind – a symbol of total exposure. That is my way of life too – the achievement of it and the danger of it. T.E. Lawrence would understand Mark's stresses but not how he commits suicide out of a passion for life. Mark can't handle passion on all fronts – he says to life, I can't cope, so reabsorb me into the elements – make me again into something else.

For weeks I've woken up every morning desperate. There's no movement anywhere, not even in myself. That's what Mark thinks, and the sentence haunts me. Nothing means much to me – I feel bitter and isolated. I've been taken over by him – but what can I do about it? – it's the only way I know how to write – by total identification. A week ago I felt bruised all over – then I went insensitive – self-protective, I suppose.

There is a peculiar defectiveness in my contacts with everyone (especially those closest) a sort of universal rejection or withdrawal I've never experienced before. If I feel nothing I'm not so bad – though the business of going on like an automaton without interests or pleasures is wearing to say the least – but if I feel at all I cry. There's no middle road. The greater proportion of pain to pleasure in all contacts makes me avoid them, while there's a part of me so outraged at the impossibility of the situation it's ready to throw in the towel, disappear or lock myself up and never come out.

Watching Willie Russell's *Educating Rita*, a film I enjoyed two years ago for its moral balance, I was overwhelmed with tears by Rita's friend, who commits suicide because she feels locked out of the rich flow of life experienced in great music and literature. I felt I was at the other end of the same broken chain – locked out by other people's inability to live at my pace or (as I fear) be really changed by my work when they read it.

Nobody knows the insecurity underlying what they call my confidence, optimism, positivity – I don't advertise it because I want to minimise it. I am a native of chaos – treading water, often joyously, not in misery like Beckett – but I've invested my security in people – Brian and Jane – and that makes me all the more vulnerable.

On our weekend in Edinburgh my misery has surfaced. I confessed, 'I seriously consider suicide' –

in such a way that Jane and Brian were really scared. They assured me theirs would follow. After an hour's desperate talk I felt different about it: 'I know I couldn't now,' I told them, 'held by these flesh ties – as if pregnant.'

My writing has brought to the surface and given body to half-buried aspects of me – created a new me. I find it uncomfortable to live with. This novel dug down into the silt below the clear stream – the story demanded it, I didn't will or expect it. It has separated me more from easy identification with others. I need – must have – compensation for that in the shape of the company of more people – more interesting people – who will be attracted by reading my work and make themselves more readily accessible because of it.

December 1983

Tessa Rushbrooke's New Year's Eve party. I wondered if it might bring back the flu I've had for the past fortnight, but no: I want to be with people – any people, not specially interesting or intelligent – and hold hands at midnight.

I got happily drunk on three monster gins – utterly relaxed, with a childlike, gentle, affectionate and laughing enjoyment of everything, even of my own discomfort in coughing or in finding that at least three others in the room (including Adam Rushbrooke) had written unpublished novels. I even laughed and nodded to another while he boasted about his poems. How lovable the men! Keith, Tessa's new partner, really comforted me when I had my coughing bout – putting his arms round me and letting me lean on him – and said afterwards how much he'd enjoyed it. I do like him – one of the most natural men I've met – and very tactile – quite sexy when he greets you with a kiss. But he makes almost no memorable impact – like a great big dog that you hug most enjoyably, push away and forget. He thinks I'm just sweet natured like himself – God knows what he'll make of my book! But I like to float incognito in other people's worlds. To be a real writer you have to have the responses of a child or an animal alongside the trained ones, and resist any attempt to impose on them or overlay them.

Tessa would be mad to drop him and go back as she says she would to Adam, whose deceptive good looks have finally deserted him, leaving him clearly tense and problematic. Keith adores her – he simply believes everything she tells him – needing to belong, he's devoted because that's the condition of belonging. And he enjoys the hectic adventure of being rushed from pillar to post of practical jobs.

I liked that big tubby grey-haired bear of a man who hardly said a word but mixed me all those gins and enjoyed their effect on me – he was comfy to lean on when he helped me up the stairs to find Brian – for I couldn't bear to be without him, even long enough for him to pee.

After supper and Auld Lang Syne Adam strummed the double bass, another man played the piano, and we all sang old pop songs.

At home as we were going to bed I joined in a fuck meant as a romp for Brian, who said, 'It never crossed my mind until I saw you naked.'

I replied, 'It never crossed mine till you got inside me!'

Remission

January 1984

I came across Orwell's statement that a writer is 'driven on by some demon he can neither resist nor understand.' I agree. There was no way of knowing consciously how this novel of mine would turn out. For instance, I started it with the conviction that salvation lay in thinking things through. My time in hospital, together with later developments in the novel itself have changed me. I more and more value the associative: diverse natures getting together, not governed relentlessly by their fixed selves but discarding the unwanted self, identifying with each other and every living thing. It's this blood-associativeness we three have so strongly that I try to achieve with others – even with people polarically different. Sympathetic identification is the only label I've found for it. People think that means something different from thought, whereas it's what thinking has to work on, work with – without it thinking is just pattern-making. In the future I want to reveal the rich potentialities locked up in everyone. The kind of achievement we normally value is a form of limitation.

When I was watching King Cong (the 1976 version) I burst into tears when Cong was gunned down at the end. I loved him – he was so much more loving than the humans – prepared to risk everything. There you see in pop terms my preference for the animal-associative.

Some people like to be one or two steps ahead in any relationship so that they can spot the exits out of tight corners. What they don't realise is that you can't learn to be really fast except by what they're always avoiding – being bundled into experiences you can't handle and learning by your suffering there.

March 1984
Bowling down the road to Banbury with our new friends, the Irwins, kids in the back of the estate car, listening to pop, whistling together (confidently out of tune) and chatting aimlessly – 'having fun!' as Graham said and I agreed. I played with Lenny (nearly five) – tickle, bite, suck and giggle. He said, 'I'm going to suck your thumb!' – and he got it all in, halfway down his throat. He was burrowing in my breast and grabbing handfuls of thigh. I modestly declined to tickle him through the hole in his pants next to his penis, though he claimed indignantly, 'Mummy does it!'

Graham and I swapped favourite Woody Allen jokes. His was, 'What's wrong with masturbation? – you're having sex with someone you love,' and mine: 'One thing you can say about God is that he's an under-achiever.' He said, about his academic research, 'I found I couldn't sit still for more than 20 minutes without wanting to go and have a wank – what I was reading or writing, I suppose, stirred me up.' That's how I feel sometimes with my writing – can't wait to get to bed afterwards – though not for wanking!

He's a congenial extravert, innocent but complicated. And he's very cuddly, like a friendly bear. I like hugging his big belly – Graham Bear I call him. He speaks directly to the kid in me. I decided some years ago that that's where all the goodies are, and to live as far as possible from there. We're alike in our animal responsiveness: we want whatever we're driven to *now, extremely,* however unimportant it is.

He said, 'I wish I could have more – eat more, fuck more, enjoy more of everything!' – and his wife Janet added, 'But I get easily sated with the physical – more excited about spiritual things.' Actually I feel like both of them – can never get enough of anything, including the spiritual. I move from one Irwin to the other, either bounced off by his restlessness or bored with her neurotic obsessions.

My reactions to him veer wildly from self-identification to rejection and back again. We come at every human relationship from opposite angles – he to beat the other person, I to love him. No, that's not the whole truth, he loves and wants to be loved, but he's so competitive. With Lenny I watched his attention-claiming turn to tickling – I identified up to that point – and then to rough-housing in which he praised his aggressiveness.

He said how much he admired Barry Humphries: 'I love energy!'

'But putting down a person like Za-Za Gabor,' I said, 'is like putting a hunchback on a wheel and laughing at him.' I went for him because he can always look after himself in an argument – there aren't many of our other friends who can. During it Janet sensed he was exposed and began to express some of the criticisms of him that she's kept pent up, unable normally to deliver them because he moves too fast out of her range. She was like my mum in a similar situation, her little fists up. But as with my parents, as soon as I saw the lid come up and a monster appear, I changed sides and supported him.

Later she told me a dream in which she saw men torturing Graham in an upstairs room. She went into the basement kitchen and found me with a paper penis – she bounced up and down on it, getting high, and rang up Amnesty International to get Graham released. I think the dream showed her getting high on the potency I represent in my writing – a new assurance, a creative power she sees as female since it's being engendered in opposition to Graham's kind of mental manipulation – the torture in the upper chamber.

April 1984
Visit to the Birmingham Botanical gardens with the Beechams.

James said I looked 'distinguished – like a don,' and talked of the 'power and truth' of my conversation. He said, 'I wish I could make a videotape of you! I find it very erotic, being in contact with a female mind.'

All that depressed me – it's another pedestal – distinction instead of the physical beauty he used to adore – that inhibits the playful intimacy I still hope for from him. I wanted to stand on my head and show my knickers to cure him of it. Instead I went in for horseplay – whistling and rude remarks – that made Claire and their daughter move away in embarrassment.

Claire's shrunken body and huge fashionable specs made her look like one of the endangered species, but for the first time I found her more interesting to talk to than James. I liked her stories of bottom-stream kids in her secondary school coming up to her with their 'small twisted faces screwed up at angle' – how they took 15 minutes to find their exercise books and then opened them at random, upside down or sideways. I sympathised when she told me on the quiet about a love affair – her first, and more rewarding sexually than her marriage. I wondered if we were going to have a friendship at last, after all these years. But she's got everything in such small quantities that I can hardly recognise them.

James told me about his new oriental religion. Making a gesture of 'surrender' in Subud style he talked of allowing Claire more life of her own. She may see that as just another gesture of cop-out! The vivid personal responsiveness that has given him so much trouble all his life is now dying on him, so he's surrendered himself to this, hoping it will grant him a sense of release without risk – but it hasn't worked.

'I can't lose myself in anything,' he said. 'I'm bored with everything – and feel guilty about my laziness.'

'Perhaps it comes,' I said, 'from forcing your feelings instead of creating the right conditions for your interest to grow.'

I discussed some general ideas with him. When he said animals don't have souls, I replied, 'Yes they do! – and so do plants – if you mean what I mean by soul: life-energy and self-sustaining individuality.' But in argument he goes through the same kind of intellectual gambits with me as my father used to. For

Dad, every argument was an exercise of the brain – a circular trot. He was like Omar Khayyam in one of his favourite quotes: 'I heard great argument, but evermore came out by the same door as in I went.' I on the other hand always want to get somewhere, test and change my ideas, explore experience.

When he said goodbye he wanted to put his arms round me, wanted the contact – yet when he did it his body went flabby, his eyes glaucous, his face deadpan. What was off-putting was the cut-out, the switching off from stimulus.

And at the last minute before leaving he told me he's suffering from rectal cancer and soon to have an operation on it. And now I'm reluctant to see him again because he's taken over the position in my imagination that Dad had before his death. When I behave towards my own horrors as if they don't exist – as I did in hospital – everybody admires the over-ride – they call it brave, noble, etc – but when I act towards other people's in the same way it's inconsiderateness – and I feel guilty too. But it is the same inescapable chemical blood-reaction in both cases.

Early May 1984
Brian's got into the habit every morning, after tea in bed, of pulling back the bedclothes, kissing my pubes, rolling me over, gently biting my bum and saying, 'Come on, get up!' Today he added, 'And give us the rest of that chapter! – I don't know which end of you I adore the most.'

But how can I make much progress when I work only half an hour a day? It's all this vacation socializing, with Jane at home all day every day. I feel confined: unable to go out for long trips without her, because she's too nervous about our safety – or out with her, because she can't spare the time from her work; unable to have our normal flow of music, conversation and cuddles; yet unable to feel towards her anything but love and willingness to serve her.

And I have to take time talking to Brian every morning, with tea in bed – must chew over the previous day's happenings, or I can't write at all. I talk away, sometimes with diminishing returns from him. 'You can yawn and prop up the wall,' I tell him, 'but I must have my say. Talking gets my chemistry going, and completing what I have to say gets it appeased. It sets my imaginative world in motion so that when I get out of bed I can step into it and not into the meaningless material world of washing, housework, eating and so on. The dumb world of practicalities is a nightmare to me – I come alive as soon as I can talk.'

This wonderful wine-like air and sunshine makes me feel brimming over with affection, talk, funfulness. I feel stronger now than I did before the operation and seem to be more attractive to men than I was when I was younger. And I'll go berserk if I don't have Brian soon! I long for those days when we're together, the two of us, and I respond to him as if by osmosis.

Late May 1984
In the afternoon we started out for a swim at the university (Jane was away) got half way, when I said, 'My fanny is saying yes to the idea of a fuck,' so we

turned back. Lying in bed naked, I watched Brian undress, his penis lengthening – like a horse's! – nothing in the world's so beautiful.

Five vivid orgasms in ten minutes – my fanny's into a ring-pulling phase. I asked Brian to have his on top, so that we could come together on my sixth – though in fact I came a few seconds before him.

'Did you enjoy us?' I said. 'Let's watch lovely old black-and-white movies for the whole evening! Since the hysterectomy sex has become altogether more relaxed and playful. I could do that all over again! I'm really learning how to enjoy being on top. I do call on the Almighty a lot while I'm coming, don't I?'

'You'll feel shagged later. I'd better ration you to an average of one orgasm a day – six today makes nine this week.'

'All right – lots of kisses then. I love kisses between fucks – it's like a recall, my fanny swells – though when I'm on the job it's a distraction I don't want.... Smell this' – I held my finger out – 'smells of my fanny. I like the smell – reminds me of good times. I had to relearn that from a chimp.'

June 1984

After reading a *Guardian* article on 'the fractal dimension' of plants and their minute inhabitants, I walked round the garden in the sunshine, dazzled by the beauty of the flowers and the thought of the fractal world. It enhances my sense of interchangeability – the distinction between one form of life and another so thin it makes the concept of death meaningless. But I also need the sense of space and freedom that ignorance gives.

In the evening a TV programme on Lovelock's Gaia theory of the way living organisms regulate the environment. I was irritated by his silly face, unsupported assumptions and anthropomorphic metaphors. Scientists are babies when it comes to words. But the interaction of the organic and inorganic appeals to me. It's the viruses I most admire (and fear) for flexibility and opportunism – they're only strips of DNA that ride on the structure of their hosts. My own tightrope theory makes out that life balances itself within tight limits – destruction either side – though within those limits with a scope for creativity that seems limitless!

July 1984

Getting into the swing of writing again. Today I've done more work in three quarters of an hour than in the whole of the past week – partly because I've accepted the slow pace. If you're all the time thinking *I must get on* you can't. If I slow down I can focus, and then the transformation takes place. It's just as important as the first stage of creation, requires just as much expertise. I take six or seven paragraphs at a time, hold them up to the light, looking at them from all angles through my jeweller's magnifying glass, chipping away at them. I get bored with them at times but I can't not do the job.

You have to lead the reader into an image the way a plant leads a bee into its flower – so that he follows the main thread into the centre and at the same time gets his back covered with associative pollen. I'll alter a sentence endlessly to find the right sound I need to enhance the meaning. When I get it just how I want it, it's more like light than speech: when you've seen things like that your vision is permanently altered. Eventually in making the final fair copy I'll hardly alter a word because if I did I'd have to consider how that one word altered the music – the rhythm, the sound effect – and that would mean reading the passage over and over – and I've done all that.

The characters in my book are peeling open like onions now – and their responses are no longer set out as separate viewpoints but plaited together. It's the plait – the interplay – which is the plot. The discussion finally gets lost in the drama – or rather, in the central portions, fused. The arguments now are like making love – two threads of thought interlocked and coming to a resolution that is neither of them.

The thing I most like about it is the way the energy keeps coming from all sides in a given situation – so many different responses to it from the different characters and a feeling that if others were introduced there would be that number of fresh angles on it. After you've finished reading my stuff I hope you feel as if you've been in Piccadilly Circus, your responses jostled and sharpened, forced to see real life with the same eyes as me. I see art as a therapy much like the exercises they give you in hospital for a damaged limb. You realise you can make these movements during the exercise, then why not in daily life?

Some people – academics especially – will say about a book, 'Yes, those are fine feelings,' but they themselves stay safe in their own skulls. In the arguments in my book – it's the only reason I do them, they give me more trouble than anything else – I want each tight, well-constructed skull to be knocked out, floored by another equally well-constructed – so that you're left only with sympathetic identification, nothing else to rely on, nothing left to limit your responsiveness.

But I'm worried that the book is too full of stress. I hope the total effect is like Mahler – stress resolved. It was always Mahler I wanted to hear after my mastectomy. But I hardly ever put one view without its opposite, and that may make everything seem undermined. I do see life as fraught with contradictions, but I see every change, however contrary to what's hoped for by our limited intelligence, as full of the unborn and I can't help loving it for that. It's the fertile anarchy I like. So I generally finish up with a sense of exuberance. It isn't just animal energy – I was like it at the lowest ebb after the operation. I see life as just as difficult as Beckett – though I don't just come up with a handful of dead leaves. He says, If life is like this it's not worth living – I say, If life weren't like this it wouldn't be worth living.

After reading part of the manuscript, Brian said, 'It makes room for people to breathe, think and respond – it's releasing and joy-giving.'

'You couldn't have said anything I more wanted to hear,' I said. 'Freedom and joy – it's all I've ever wanted – and what I have normally – though no-one looking at my way of life would think so!'

September 1984
Lunch with Humphrey Green at St John's College. With three other Fellows in their panelled room, we had two waiters to serve six of us. The silver bowl of

fruit raised on a slim stem in front of Humphrey's nose looked so much like a Dutch still life it seemed arrogant to take some – but that's just about the measure of the place. The room had a life of its own, but the men in it seemed to me cocky, plundering, sealed off. That doesn't mean I wasn't curious – I liked their physical presence – but not the brittle assurance.

Humphrey isn't brittle – too confident in his dreams. I like his enthusiasm, emotionality – the general urge towards life and 'goodness' as he sees it, that isn't as silly and sentimental in him as it might be. I used to be intrigued and attracted by the combination of aesthete and rugger player in him – the sensitive, small hands of a violinist but with black hairs growing vigorously on their backs, a pallor and nervousness, a certain 'book' damage done to his physique by his academic career, conflicting – no, not conflicting, living alongside – considerable physical robustness. His bright keen hazel eyes and grey and black hair captured my imagination and became an aspect of a portrait that found its way into *The Commune.*

Ten years ago the conflict was active, he was struggling. Now that sense of pent-up power has deserted him – his face is still mobile and sensitive but 'distinguished' instead of punchy. He still has his mixture of arrogance and humility – but the courage has degenerated into foolhardiness, at least as regards some of his opinions. That panting, impetuous emotionality, without any outlet but the cultural, has made a nutter of him. His intellect never was strong enough for it – he couldn't get the two in harness. And he no longer wants real living. He wants to be the owner of originals, like Weinberger's paintings, and the owner of originality, like his protégée the poetess.

He tells us that, under the influence of Attenborough's *Ghandi* film, he's decided to reduce his income so as to pay no tax to a government he doesn't approve of – donating the surplus to charity – so he puts up with the poverty of his rooms, his paintings and his meals in college! He says he feels 'an urgency to declare myself,' and dreams of founding a 'House' where everyone lives simply, and it's to be filled with all the 'saintly' women he meets – he knows lots! One beautiful lawyer he met he 'very nearly fell desperately in love with.' How do you very nearly fall desperately in love? Unfortunately Humphrey's salvation lies in celibacy, so he says. He wants to encourage life by recoiling from it – basically this giving up of salary is just another giving up, like giving up his wife and family and sex – though his love of life is such he'd die for it – I'm sure he'd be grateful to – it's living that's hard.

The afternoon was a terrible strain. Most of the time I was tormented with not wanting to hurt his feelings by coming out with what I thought about his ideas. As he left us, hugging himself – characteristic gesture – the picture of isolation, I felt touched, compassionate, and perhaps I let him see it – if so, he won't easily forgive me.

In the night I dreamt of being pulled out of swamps. He haunts me with his appeal – that bathroom of his, with its pictures of Mickey Mouse and Donald Duck, some badly washed socks and a jock strap is such a picture of personal destitution.

Brian said, 'If only he believed in a few Christian tenets, there's nothing he'd like more than to put on a Friar's cloak, tie a rope round his middle and walk the streets of Cambridge in sandals.'

My own fantasy of him is as a Welsh preacher pitching his tent on the hillsides for a rapt few until some randy teenager tears off his jock strap and he says, 'I didn't mean that kind of love – you don't understand' – when she's the only one who does!

'One more person I'm disappointed in,' I said when we got home.

'You make them up,' said Jane.

'When they wear trousers!' Brian added.

April 1985

Renoir exhibition. Wonderful to find someone who responds like me! It isn't just the few men I look at – or the women in relation to them – there's that fiery gipsy girl I like, and the landscape at Wargemont with its fluidity – the chaos of surging life – it seems to change shape as you alter your viewpoint.

There was a TV programme on Renoir recently, in which the 'experts' gave barbed or grudging praise and quoted him in a sugary voice. I was ashamed and disgusted at the whole thing – with those magnificent paintings giving the lie to everything those ball-less, gutless creatures said. I love Renoir mainly for those paintings where men appear – he's as good as Titian at depicting maleness and the magnetism between the sexes, as in his dancing pictures. Pity he was so obsessed with the female – if I were a painter we'd see the tables turned! He so needed the peace he saw in her – you can see in his self-portrait how exposed he was – emotionally intense, unstable, fraught – it's the basis from which he constructed his images of harmony and balance – the compulsion behind their perfection.

Jean Renoir reported that his father treated religious and social beliefs as 'only the outward workings of individuals,' whom he classified chiefly according a difference between those who perceive and those who reason. 'And the brain itself is an ugly thing – it has no value but what you put into it,' he said.

I couldn't agree more – to all of that. He saw through the pretensions of opinion. I know from my own experience how easily the resultant tolerance or indifference can be mistaken for a simpleton's. When you've got no opinion on Big Issues – because to you they're non-issues – people assume you can't think at all. I like the way whatever Renoir said 'depended on the people he happened to be with at the time' and I completely understand that as an artist he 'only wanted to be a mechanism to take in and give out.'

October 1985
Picasso exhibition. He's like James Joyce – powerful intellectuality, equally powerful sensuality. Their confinement to and concentration on those areas set free or set going all that technical exploration. I'm often tempted, as I am with Joyce, to dismiss him for his poor emotional equipment – an insensitivity to people based on a limited range of response in himself – but like Joyce the powers he has are so strong they work up complex effects. I respond to him as to something other – I don't identify much. And such a male! – look at his photo: young bull – and later old

goat. When a friend asked why I chose to bring home a postcard of *Figures au bord de la mer,* which he called coarse, I replied, 'I like coarse sometimes.' I liked even more the *Minotaur's Embrace* for its combination of ferocity and tenderness.

I've heard how Picasso diversified his sexual activities in his forties, taking on two women for a number of years, and I understand that. By this age you're thoroughly confident in your animal life, and sex is the experience that makes life indisputably right. I'm appreciative of maleness in all its variations now more than ever – except the juvenile and the neurotic. I remember in an Oxford street recently passing a young man bending to look in a shop window, I could scarcely refrain from squeezing his bum!

In the film *Chariots of Fire* I loved all that young, vigorous male flesh, and automatically discounted the Boy's Own element, but what really got me as usual was the achievement bit. I identified with each of the world-beaters so hard I couldn't tell whether I felt most like the one who did it out of delighted energy and religious idealism – running for the animal and the god in him – or the one who was proving his own personal power in defiance of what was established.

January 1986
Singing with Jane the hits from *Evita* – 'High-flying adored' and 'I'd be surprisingly good for you.'

Brian said, 'Why do you go in for that crap?'

'Jenny puts me in touch with the public's response, throws me into the stream of their consciousness. I'm not going to lose contact with that or with her by being critical. Anyway, she reads into it only the fairytale, without the politics. She identifies both herself and me with Evita as the embodiment of female life-giving strength. She has a fresh, open and crude response to life – how I value that! The more she achieves autonomy in the running of her life the more assured I feel of her continuing connection with us. I don't miss authority and supervision – never really wanted it.'

Jane is easy to get on with recently, particularly when I'm under stress (she's scared of my illness or breakdown): helpful in the house and really good company when we're out together. A bit irritable at times – always a few jagged edges with her – but she likes riding on my back – on my highs, at least. I think it's because she now feels completely accepted and welcomed at home, not alternately loved and rejected as she was after the breakdown of her last affair. She still regards me, of course, not as a person with needs of my own but like a supply of oxygen. She wants me to be a Genii, slave of the lamp – she rubs it and I appear to perform the tasks she can't – so long as I go back into the lamp again!

Sometimes in the shops I can't make contact with her – if she's obsessed with trying on pair after pair of trousers and worrying about the chipmunk pouches on her thighs. A thousand different ways to deform your figure! In the street she manages me much like Brian. Once, bowling along, happy as a sand boy, I moved out into the road to avoid some dustbins and she hauled me back by my collar-scarf, shouting, 'Where are you going, you stupid arsehole!' – more like an irate father than a daughter.

Nowadays if she comes home from work tired, depressed and irritable, I can persuade her on to the lounge couch – her usual position, full length with her feet over one end, head on my thigh, held round the waist and facing the box – and after an hour or so of that she's quite a different girl. Yesterday we watched *Showboat* as if with one pair of eyes. The tensions between us peeled off like layers of an onion. I had my baby back, I felt warm – protected and protecting – two bloodstreams flowing as one.

She took us to supper at Raymond Blanc's Manoir as a way of celebrating her new job and my clean bill of health. We were amazed at the flavours but disappointed at the amount (main course: tiny pigeon, one sprout, a cabbage leaf, a fragment of parsnip, half a potato chip, a mushroom and a spoonful of mashed chestnut). The purism of the man! It's like unsatisfied sex. Perhaps he never does more than lick his fingers: oh sprout, with my tongue I thee worship. But one day when he comes round to see how discriminating his guests have been, someone will black his eye.

I prefer our Saturday suppers, where we toast 'Us forever!' and 'The Future!' I'm in danger of wanting three of everything – when I'm writing, if I can think of three reasons or three aspects I never look for more!

March 1986
Manchester. I'm here out of curiosity about Lowry's background and to locate an extra site for my next novel. Beetling about in the cold. Because the buildings dwarf you and there are wide bleak spaces of light and flat black ground between them, you

focus more on your inner life, inner warmth, inner objectives.

Eating in a vegetarian restaurant feels like dangerous living when the knives and forks slip out of your hand from other people's grease. The intellectuals and health freaks frequenting it are mixed students and adults. One or two fluffy-sweatered gays but mostly nose-to-the-trough family bods, exchanging timetables or feeding kids. Intellectualism expressed more in nervous irritability. One man came back from the counter three times to feed his kids – snapping at them from three yards away and wiping every soup bowl and plate on my head as he passed. The room was packed for maximum sitting: long shiny pine much-spilt-on tables and benches. We found one of the very few small tables for 2-4 people. Steamy windows. No name over the front – could be a launderette from the outside but has managed to find its way into the *Good Food Guide*. Can't see why but it does make the most of a few vegetables.

Next day we walked around the city centre – Quay Street and Bailey Bridge. Some of sky the colour of concrete – the rest of it brilliant blue. The light comes all over the buildings, making them look more important than anything else. Neolithic blocks with spaces round them. Old LNER goods offices looking a bit like a prison, but Dickensian, attractive. A city dedicated to great structures. The impression of hard work and the grimness of life but at the same time tremendous vigour. On the bridge the motto *Industry and Integrity* with what looks like a cross between a lion and a wolf. The river Irwell like a black mirror. The people toothy, hairblown, what-are-you-doing-mate – not aggressive or surly in cliques as in London or Birmingham – not insular. They look at you a bit like starlings.

The Salford Art gallery was crowded (Sunday) with people interested in the photo exhibition (pictures of Salford) and the reconstructed Victorian street. In the Lowry room I became saturated with his particular view of life – the loneliness, toughness, vividness, vigour – the way in which he describes even the cripples with a tremendous purchase on life – strength and comedy in almost everyone's movement and gesture. In *The Cripples* there's such energy and attack, and no sentimental pity – that's how I felt about the tramps in London. In *The funeral Party* the first woman on the right looks as if she doesn't know why she's there, the next one as if she knows very well, it's the right thing – and what's going on between the boy and girl?

I passed quickly over *The Lake 1937* – a vision of hell – to enjoy most of the industrial landscapes, especially *An Accident* and *Coming from the Mill*. Finding out that Lowry felt 'rapture' at such scenes, I agreed – that's how I feel. Coming out into Peel Park I found my own feelings superimposed on top of Lowry's and the whole thing suddenly becoming bright and joyous.

Driving out towards the motorway, under a hard bright sky with high white clouds, the local streets and buildings were vividly recognisable: a Lowry sense of confinement. Buildings bashed up against each other – a feel of aggression between them, or sometimes warm intimacy: too close yet wonderfully close. That kind of friction – the two extremes – comes out in his scenes and to some extent in the faces of the people he painted. Humour and compassion – no cynicism or contempt.

September 1986

Mammogram at Selly Oak Hospital. A waiting room with four semi-corpses in wheelchairs – hell would be a pantomime after that! – and a cubicle where I have to strip naked and put on a dressing-gown still warm from another's body.

A long bath at home. My fear gets fixated on objects that can be removed or washed away; the alternative is to stare it straight in the face.

After a good sleep with nitrazepam, I woke without aches and temperamentally calm. I need this peace agent – wish it weren't addictive. People say it makes them sleepy the next morning – it just makes me happy – normal – without stress. Is this what some people feel like all the time? – lucky sods!

By the afternoon my emotions were plunging and soaring as usual – very excited about the thriller on tv. By the evening I was played out – too tired even to turn off that shitty Horson Smelles film.

Jane said, 'How do you stand this way of life, with dinner so late in the day there's never time for anything but telly afterwards. You spend your entire life, Mum, getting up and going to bed!'

'She's right, you know,' Brian said. 'An hour getting to breakfast and another from breakfast to work – and longer still at bedtime.'

'But I need the dreaming time – it's like an athlete limbering up – otherwise I'd never write as I do, I'd make mistakes that I'd have to correct the next day. I need to be unerring, so I need the limbering up. As for the tv, I'm potentially a junky and telly's my junk. I get tired of constantly managing my demanding personality – it's a relief to be drugged out of it. Some nights nowadays, though, I'm so plastered I feel I'm in a dark tunnel and wonder how I'm going to get through all the cleaning and creaming rituals I have to do before I can go to bed.'

Brian said, 'Don't do it – it's only a neurotic compulsion.'

'Only! – that's why I have to do it.'

The slightest exertion nowadays and I'm flogged. I'm so susceptible to shock and surprise – even the sight of strong emotions or conflict on the screen – that I long to interpose a lymph-like layer between me and the world. Any physical effort – gardening, fucking, swimming or even sitting tense writing – gives me aches in muscles and joints – I can rattle my foot joints like castanets sometimes! That's why I go sometimes several days without physical exercise, and even miss out on the restorative joy of coming in my fucks, which take so long because I'm so tired to start with. They exhaust me sometimes – after the last one I felt as if my sinews were all strung out like a dressed chicken's. Headache on the first orgasm: excruciating – like the cramps I used to get in my legs – though I know now that it'll go with the second or third.

Anyway, I'm so tired because the aches won't let me sleep properly beyond five o'clock. I never relax nowadays, even in bed or telewatching.

I'm grateful to Jane for finding in a book that some of these symptoms are typical of the climacteric. She must be right. Sometimes the most excruciating aches,

like the ones I had at the cinema the other day will
subside almost to nothing after wine and a good meal
and chatting funfully – taken out of myself.
Sometimes I get up happy and energetic – with the
muscular flexibility of a five-year-old! – but later in
the day, especially after listening to Jane's current
anxieties, every muscle aches – it's like clockwork,
that reaction to stress. I'm depressed at the thought of
the next few years crocked like this, exhausted by
multiple sweats and not in normal contact.

Yesterday afternoon I went alone on our three mile
circular walk with headphones playing *Taras Bulba*.
Sealed off in my inner world – the music organising it
– happy to be so. Recently I quickly tire of human
contact – I'm especially rejective of Jenny's. I can't
continuously give out what she needs every second of
her being with me – warmth and security, and the
disentangling of her confusions. Perhaps in my next
book I'll protect myself more from the glare of reality
– go in for a Dickensian or Renoirish insistence on
warmth of feeling.

May 1987
Finals exhibition at the local art college. Reception
afterwards. Junked up room, filthy, people used to
getting messed up and feeling perhaps it gives life a
kind of intimacy hard to come by in any other way –
but it could be equally representative of mess and
chaos inside looking for some kind of form on canvas.
The mature students' faces almost universally gentle,
verging towards weak and cop-out – but a few
'assertives' either in dress (cropped head and earring)
or guarded, 'fuck-you' look. Non-posing behaviour

with each other – good, 'sensitive soul' vibes. The expression this takes in their art is impressionability to the teacher and each other. All the products are blood relatives – the melodramatic 'Munch' look (obviously the teacher's favourite) is universal. With all the struggle towards self-expression and individuality, that is what's most noticeably missing.

We went home with the Irwins. Graham was there in his baggiest clothes, his little eyes shrunk behind tinted glasses, and his new swept-back hairdo. 'Take me as I am,' he seemed to be saying – but what was he at that moment but repulsively self-indulgent? Making cups of tea, he handed them first to his kids, then to his wife, then to us. I got the last mug, so chipped I could hardly find a place for my mouth.

He was throwing up a stink barrier. I saw in his eyes not only tiredness and *Leave me to myself* but mistrust of me – partly because of my 'demanding' nature, and partly perhaps because he's read in *The Commune* that I'm not the kind of woman he hoped I was. Anyway I felt he was doing a number on me.

He lay back on the sofa with his feet on his wife's lap and launched into a 'therapeutic' challenge to my anxieties: 'Why do you think the world is going to destroy you?'

'I don't – but I sometimes feel, if it produces any more hassle I'll destroy myself!'

He was pleased at what he called my embarrassment, but I was confused rather than embarrassed. If any one builds a sufficiently watertight case – an island for me to stand on and look at myself – I'll do it. For a moment I was that immature, frightened person he was describing. After that I was suppressing retaliatory comments that might hurt him.

He talked of writing fiction himself and needing fine paper and a custom-built book, with an assortment of interesting pens, to write down his thoughts. I tried desperately to switch tracks as usual, to get my train of responses going in the direction his were taking so as to enjoy his scenery, but they obstinately refused. He was too tired to yank me on board and I was too tired to do all the work myself.

After admitting they felt 'too old to stay up late,' he and Janet groused about their Aged P's, now in their eighties, who have nothing to talk about but the people they see on telly – naturally, poor sods, they don't meet anyone else! Anyway, if they get tired of Felicity Kendall they can always switch to another channel – I wished I could at that moment!

Then I felt guilty, remembering his generosity. When he brought us a carload of books from Charles Monteith's library (having set us up as book dealers because we were short of money) 'All yours for £350!' he said, and rapidly explained how we could double it. I realised that for him, as for my mum, practical generosity is a way of relating. I'm so sorry I never understood fully enough with her – always rejected it – but with Graham I'll repay him in kind – give him his choice of my manuscripts – and I must have him in my next novel!

People call him charismatic, and yes, what makes people charismatic is the perfect conjunction of their nature with the codes they're operating. Graham's nature is variable, dispersed in different directions – his antennae, his tentacles latch on to the needs of those he's dealing with and manipulate them according to the business code. About that – and about everything beyond family and close friends – there is in him a profound cynicism, but not depressive or unsettling – presumably because he feels he can cope with such a world and get what he needs from it. But his egoism is like a plait you can never unweave.

July 1987

Last week I went with Jenny to the Regal to see Badham's *Short Circuit*: the best film I've seen in ages! The tears ran off my chin – and I laughed a lot too. I madly identified with the robot. It's the malfunction – when he's struck by lightning, making him useless for conventional purposes – that makes him a genius among robots. He's so lovable – hates death ('disassembly') so much – and he's hunted, killed, resurrected and takes refuge among those who love him – what gorgeous symbolism! I loved his insatiable 'Input! input! – malfunction – input!' When I told Brian this he said, 'Sounds like you in bed.'

This week I saw the film again, with him and our closest friend, Douglas. Sitting between those two sober sides it wasn't exciting or funny or amusing, but silly and obvious – the four-year-old in me replaced by the sceptical adult.

At home afterwards I found myself thinking, Why am I sitting here with these two farts? They're both insentient in different ways – when I'm cross I call Brian a clod and Douglas a jerk. One with his scepticism about whether racoons like classical music, the other with his tale of the budgie who liked it at least as much as the vacuum cleaner. And all evening

I sat in a shower of sweat – I went to the loo partly to escape them and partly to mop up the wet.

Douglas's nature is trickier and more inaccessible than Brian's (I've woven aspects of it into the portrait of Joan in *The Commune*). When he brought gifts from his holiday in Greece, a large photo of the head of Poseidon and a copy of some dolphins from Knossos, 'Absolutely spot-on!' I said – 'just what I'd have chosen. Get up, I feel so grateful I must express it.' And I gave him a hug. But he just wasn't there – stood like a block, a brown totem pole. I felt as I would if I'd been drunk and taken in my arms a tree stump shaped like a man. It was a physical shock – as an animal must feel if it accidentally puts a stone in its mouth thinking it's food. A complete absence – or suppression – of animal energy.

Occasionally I feel rejective of him, especially since he failed to react with any enthusiasm to my draft of *The Commune*. Then I see him waiting passively for understanding and love, assuming they're earned by the passivity – trying to make a virtue out of a restraint that comes easier to him than anything else. On a trip last month to Chipping Campden it was like going out with my dad. He asked about all the people we'd met and with an Oh yes about each news item went back to his tuneless, almost unconscious whistling. I always know what stone he's under when he's exhausted – but he's always under some stone. What a monkish academic life he leads! – but he prefers the isolation – fed up with retaining himself but terrified of losing himself, of being hurt. How can you get interested and involved without being exposed and possibly hurt?

Then one day he'll present Ariel instead of Caliban – all air and trees and birds – and we'll be in tune again. Our weekly phone call lasts at least an hour. We tell each other about the events of the previous few days. I say, 'Got any stories to tell me?' – and he builds into a tale whatever's happened to amuse or irritate him. It's his only opportunity to share and develop or just dispose of the kind of stimulus that doesn't last more than a few days. And for me it's a tentacle, a feedback into the working world.

I enjoy his two kids, Lizzie aged sixteen and Robert eleven. When they were nippers we used to romp together.

The other day Lizzie dropped in for a couple of hours.

'I'll talk about boys,' she told me, 'to anyone who'll listen. Who've you got a crush on at the moment?'

'Er.... Ian Charleson – you know, the actor –'

'Oh yes, he's nice!'

I find her so restful to be with, it's like sleep – I really relish it when I'm frazzled. I have to guard against discounting her various attachments simply on the grounds of their being so low-key. She told me her favourite holiday so far was the one on the Norfolk broads. When I pointed out, 'But you stayed in your room most of the time,' she replied, 'Yes, but it was a room on a boat.' It was for her an imaginative experience – living a fantasy – but of a kind that didn't at first register in my mind.

I'm amazed at my patience with her! – though I can't stick at her level for long – all about Boyd the sixth former and Mr Mason the maths master – but I didn't want to cut her out so I romped with her on the couch, teasing and tickling. Sixteen she may be but still a big kid.

August 1987
Trip with Ingrid Kent and her new man, Steve Wright, to Wightwick, near Wolverhampton. I enjoyed it again – wouldn't mind returning – there's so much to see – paintings, photos, fabrics – all related to a particular group of family and friends and the culture they shared.

After a meal at the Chung Ying in Birmingham we went to the Triangle cinema to see Epstein's *The Times of Hervey Milk*, a documentary about a homosexual San Francisco town councillor killed by a colleague who got only five years in goal. It missed all its real opportunities – like all the documentaries I've ever seen – which lay in exploring the individuals concerned, the killer as well as the victim. You can't change people's understanding of these issues unless you make them identify their own motives in the characters – otherwise you simply confirm them in their present attitudes.

On the train home a black railway guard travelling off duty passed around some leaflets about his union's dispute over one-man trains. I liked the look of the man and I warmed to Steve, in his workman's jeans, feeling solidarity with him. That sense of brotherhood in a struggle for justice and equality is in my background too – I'm no less working-class than Steve and Ingrid.

Friendliness with them is so easy and natural. I warm towards Ingrid's desire for cosy permanency – hearth and home – 'reading aloud by the fire,' as she said – Darby and Joan. I envy them their securities. It's funny to see him jumping up all the time to clear away and wash up after supper – as if he's got a square arse – joking about his role – this his 'only contribution' to the household economy. He spends his whole life treading the rope of his Labour theories, and if Ingrid throws him a few extra ones he's quite happy to tread those too – afraid of the spaces between.

But sharing with him presents a problem: politics is the only subject that makes his eyes light up – on any other he's a clam. He's not much interested in personal relationships – given up the one-to-one in order to cultivate the mass relationship (I'm the opposite). He digs a moat around himself – that's where he feels cosy and where he feels in touch with the cause – and he'll throw drawbridges to you even if you're not in the Party – but 'at the end of the day' (as he's always saying) he draws them up.

I can see he's worried that we don't join the Labour Party. It's like an animal that finds we have the right smell and wonders why we're not in the pack. He wanted me to help him with his press handouts. But I'm quite incapable of writing anything without rethinking it from scratch – and he wouldn't like that! He gets me anxious and guilty about situations that are fraught with misery and menace, but in politics I can never be sure which direction to take – except for myself.

I remember his performance at a public meeting with the parliamentary candidates in the election this summer. The church hall was packed out – fun time for all. Nearly everyone a paid-up member of one or other of the parties. Intellectual football match with rowdy support, all teams playing by the unscrupulous rules of the game: doing down the others to make themselves look good and interpreting everything according to the Party gospel. A row of Tory wives all looking like Mrs Thatcher – expressions, hair-do, two-pieces, the lot. 'Answer the question!' coming from all parties to all candidates even when the question was daft. Vicar introducing – serenely wet with 'good.'

The Conservative was fat, smiling, certain of victory – 'Stop smiling, Jim,' someone shouted – bragging about his six sons – 'You're so virile, Jim!' Devious – anything goes, so long as you win.

The Liberal had severe handicaps. Obviously been to a public school. Awful posh accent, silly-ass smile, giggles and wriggles on the rostrum, but articulate, *au fait* with his materials – knew the law (was a barrister).

Steve had polished his Lancashire accent – trying hard to bridge the gap education had brought about between himself and his lost class. An isolate/dreamer with a warm heart, he was mentally further removed from his audience than the other two. He was more exposed, more on his own than them, and answered therefore more like a good man than an effective politician. He wanted to represent the masses, while being hopelessly individual. The other two while standing in their different ways for individual expression helplessly belonged to a group.

I love human beings as individuals but when they act collectively, I fear and loath them – it's always the lowest motive they act on – trained and blinkered. Yet how can they survive without some kind of collective action? It's the main theme of my book. In the film, *For King and Country*, that I saw recently, I so much preferred the victim's kind of stupidity to that of the men who killed him as a deserter and thought themselves superior. They knew less of what life's about. It was as if they were killing life itself. I am drawn more and more to those who are incompetent in the world but rooted in life – helplessly activated by instinctive feelings.

October 1987

Evening with Tessa Rushbrooke and her kids. She's more like a character out of Dickens than anyone I know. We're expected to admire the prowess of her cooking tea for 40 persons, her teaching 'at the university' – i.e. teachers on secondment – and all her sons. I was amused at her lugging her brood like Mother Courage everywhere – even on the honeymoon with Keith.

I shared for a while four-year-old Nigel's comic book, pointing out the big teeth and knobbly knees, and stroking his hair and shoulders – I could have done with more of that! – and joined Justin, now seventeen, in singing a Handel song. I loved his dear, sweet young man's voice. I noticed his ability to escape without suffering, into the institutional, the approved performance at school and so on – and I used to dislike that in him, but now he's chosen music, an escape world I can so easily share, it moved me. I enjoyed singing with him.

But I couldn't be myself – they'd all have thought me a freak. Will I ever be accepted straight off – able to be myself, have fun – without a five-year initiation? I thought my novel one day would be a bridge – it may turn out to be a gulf.

The gulf has always been there. I was sitting in a British Home Stores canteen recently listening to a couple of women disagreeing vaguely about the age of a boy they knew – was it 12 or 13? – with long pauses before they repeated identical remarks: 'His mum said....' countered by 'She's got three and he's the middle one.' Wide open spaces in their heads. The sort of women Alan Bennett writes about: he's a miserable sod – I see in him mainly a sneer with a whimper underneath – but some of his snapshot realism makes me curl up in embarrassed recognition of the idiotic meanness of the sort of people I grew up with. I used to find it frightening stupidity – preferred not to listen but watch faces and imagine what was going on inside. Now on the whole I'm braver – or perhaps I'm such a nervous tick now, that kind of vacancy has an appeal – what peace to lapse out in those long pauses, reassured by the feel of a cup in your hand! But the pack assurance meted out to me – 'Oo-er – what a freak!' – frightens me now as it always did.

Occasionally I can tune in. Shopping in Birmingham the other day with Jane I was happily chatting with the assistants. 'What's that lovely smell?' said one – 'It's these oils,' I said, 'have a sniff.' Shopping is about the only social activity I have. The assistants accept me as someone like themselves simply because I'm performing a function for them. It's a rare treat.

March 1988

Yesterday I was cooking tea, harassed by pressures from Jane's anxieties and Brian's superintendence. A plate of food fell on the floor, I exploded in anger at him. He felt (he said later) deprived of my love, and then angry, turned the desire to punish me on to himself and punched the wall, cracking a bone in his hand and feeling both self-pity and self-disgust as keenly as the physical pain. As usual when this kind of thing happens, the appeal for pity failed:

'You damaged something that belongs to me,' I said, 'you damaged me. I reacted accordingly – stress and dissociation – like an accident trauma.'

Today, with Brian out of action for housework, I'm miserable at the prospect of being swamped in chores. I have fits of aversion towards him. I want to throw his glasses down the stairs, I suspect him of dissatisfactions he won't acknowledge. His nature is so different from mine, I can't immediately identify – I haven't the input sockets, any more than he has for my manic streak – and I'm too unbalanced to objectify him as a person, to watch him and work him out and handle him as I handle everyone else. Everything then would be like treading water! No, he's like the air I breathe, I've got to take him on absolute trust. When that security is threatened I feel lost, alienated – and angry with him for bringing it about.

But sometimes exasperated, I do attack:

'How do you get by with so little talk – is your mind a blank?'

'How do you do anything else,' he said, 'when you talk so much? And where would you be if I were a blatherer instead of a listener?'

'But you meet all my anxieties recently with blankness.'

'That's meant to calm you.'

'Seal yourself off, more like. Your eyes glaze over when I'm speaking to you. So complacent, you never really listen. You live too much in the head. You wrap yourself up in your mattress of insulation and disappear into your diary – recycling our waste.'

'But the diary is mostly about you – it's an expression of my love.'

'Oh, I know, but that's part of your problem maybe – it builds up resentment because you have no life apart from me – and it's my problem too because you feed off me without feeding me back. I feel trapped in the domestic routine you've devised. We have a more boring life than anyone I know.'

June 1988

Anne, Jane's new friend, is staying with us while recovering from a light heroin trip. I like fooling around with her – calling to a grasshopper on the ceiling, 'Glasshoppa!' in a mock-Chinese voice from the TV Kung Fu series – she's in stitches. It's the sort of game I used to play with my father – very blood-relaxing. My mum thought we were insane – so does Jane most of the time. Going bananas – scatty high-jinks – is the only way I know of being as friendly as Anne wants, of making her happy.

Watching the film *The Wreck of the Mary Deare*, where Charlton Heston strips off, glistening with sweat, shovelling coal into the furnace, the two girls shouted in chorus, 'I'll have him!'

'It's no good,' I said, 'I've had him already!'

At teatime they secretly taped the conversation. I twigged there was something odd going on: 'Both of you keep looking at me,' I said, 'and then pissing yourselves. What's the matter with me? – what is it? – have I got something on my nose?... Oh please, you've got to tell me – I'm not going to speak to you till you tell me. Brian, they keep laughing at me – are my eye bags enormous or something?... Please, Jenny, what is it? – it's ever so disturbing.'

Playing the tape back afterwards they fell about in hysterics at me sounding 'like a loony' and Brian 'gormless.'

She and Jane were joking about fellatio – calling spunk in the mouth 'tadpoles' and 'snot!' I'm amazed – it's as if Jane's been two-faced – with such a squeamish horror of milk, porridge, vomit, yet able to do this, which I couldn't ever.

Anne rattled on about this and that – the umpteen people she's met, how her foot itched and her fork broke. Her lifestyle is so different from mine, her mind so juvenile, that every piece of her mosaic she places in position peels off a bit of mine. Putting herself together she unwinds me!

She stayed the night but in the morning I was keen for Madam Hassle to go home. She was making what Jane calls her baby noises, squeaks of anxiety – she saw I was distant, and flung her arms round me, asking what was wrong. My skin burned where she touched but I cuddled her and explained that I was physically tired – she accepted that. Then I had to go out and scrub my arms to rid myself of the contact! Her obsessional craving for comfort and security through animal contact is too demanding for me.

But she's right about the response to touch. If a man just brushes against my bum in a queue, accidentally or not – or if a male friend, even someone I don't much like, puts his hand on my stomach as he passes, I get a sexual response. Even if an old runt of a trolley-pusher in Sainsbury's puts his arm round me helpfully to lead me somewhere I feel all warm and cosy.

Horsing around with her got her wires crossed – affection roused her sexuality – and having to repress it made her aggressive, so tickling turned to pinching – it really hurt, so I hit back. She got up and thumped the wall.

She confessed her obsession, emotional as well as sexual, with Jane.

'It's no use,' I told her, 'thinking the obsessionalism will die out of its own accord. It may in relation to Jane but will recur with others, unless you think your way through it. You don't want to go through life leaving small piles of ashes, do you? The underlying purpose of your obsession, it seems to me, is not contact but the opposite – to push up barriers, to reject the other person and reinforce the fixed pattern, your conviction that close personal contact is a source of pain, that you can't trust people because they let you down. We want to help you understand it, to bring you closer. Don't go too far away, don't brutalise yourself with travel and hard labour in the effort to forget.'

She makes me feel that we're all flotsam on the face of the earth. That's how she is: 'Ooh, look at that!... Touch this!' – or she floats off into her pop music. No basic securities – looking for something she missed as a child – abandoned as a baby, brought up in an orphanage – and therefore can never have. She can't handle close relationships – finds herself veering in panic between demands for total possession and threats of total abandonment. But her only chance of happiness is to keep trying.

Perhaps she doesn't want to be cured – even if it's possible. Perhaps like a plant in a crevice with not enough life-drive to hang on, she'll be blown away one day by the wind. I wouldn't blame her.

Autumn 1988
Jane and her boyfriend George have decided to set up home, somewhere within walking distance.

I sometimes suspect he's an impassive depressive who comes to our house for what he calls a shot in the arm. He wants to be cosied up on the nipple of life. Whenever they quarrel, my negative capability operates on her behalf – I absorb her stress. I keep crying – little storms of tears. Her feeling that she's losing me through this new commitment makes me feel I'm losing myself: I'm 58 – nearly 60, nearly finished!. And I feel guilty about my effect on Jane – my contribution to her troubles. I've got a big ego always on the push.

Going over her options with her, I included the one involving our all moving into a big house and living together, with baby and with or without husband, and as I did so I felt peace flowing through her poor taut body and into mine. That promise inside her may give her the confidence to build the relationships she needs. What she is most afraid of is separation from us.

I do have a warm loving feeling for George – he's like a bear who's found his honey pot – and I must feed the feeling regularly by real interchange with him, spending time, having fun, chatting – or else I rage at the erosion of our relationship with Jane. The other morning I went into their bedroom, irritated with him for hanging around – so that we couldn't start our day – and he turned his face towards me like a spaniel with its ears down, and instinctively my hand came out – instead of my boot! – and I stroked his head. I've never known anyone have quite that effect – it's his ace! I sat on the bed, with him on the floor and his arm across my thigh holding me there while he sucked a pencil and listened to my reassurances over the quarrel he'd had with Jane – and Jane stroked my hair out of gratitude.

He goes for what he finds here – what has the rest of the world done for him but give him cause to slit his wrists? Over the main life-issues I respect him more than our intellectual friends. Why have a brain if you can't use it on the things that matter? Academics in their darkrooms! – switching on all sorts of artificial lights – why don't they try daylight? It would spoil the negative!

He's got the confidence now to speak freely about his breakdown and his life on the kibbutz. It's because of the individuality of his intelligence that he's run into trouble, unable to conform – and now he runs to the affection and the freedom to be himself that we offer. I think good nature is the ultimate intelligence.

February 1989
The Commune is completed.

When I'm sitting in a café, it's mainly the men I watch and want to know about. Men represent life to me – the only way I have, being without religion or politics or work, of being put in touch with a wider world – something mystical as well as sexual. I want the warmth and free flow of friendly intercourse. But I run to any call – I can never be sure it won't be more interesting than what I am doing or proposing to do at that minute. I've no self-determination – no self to determine! Some people glorify with that word their inability to respond.

The other day I watched a documentary about a female dolphin in a Brittany bay. She was playing with the scientist like a human with a kitten. When she was quivering at the patterns of light and sound in the water it looked, as he said, like ecstasy. That's what must be going on in a dolphin's cerebral cortex. We use ours to make things – building sources of security and harmony, the sciences and arts – refugees from raw experience. Dolphins find them in the raw. I enjoyed seeing her playing in the sea turbulence round the rocks – like a jacuzzi – and was impressed by the calm authority with which she escorted a shark off her territory. I wish we were more like her, more exploratory.

I desperately need new horizons.

I dream of writing a different kind of novel entirely, packed with observation of scenes and masses of minor characters. I want five plots interwoven. I'll read Dickens – he can teach me about plot, drama and entertainment – I want to appeal as he did to a wide audience – and enjoy the rewards, as he did! – and going around, looking at people and places, feeding on them. I get intensely excited about different ways of life – motor mechanics, for instance, or that builder over the road who whistles while he works. And more mental worlds too – the scientist, the social historian. What a relief it would be to be out of the literary world and mind, where everything is so known, they're all shaped by the same template. I can feel what anyone and everyone feels when I'm going to write about it – my writing enables me.

March 1989

Looking at cave paintings from the Dordogne. Quintessential! So fresh! – they make Monet look artificial. So objective, it's not like art but anti-art. The one personal and human element in it – reverence – appeals to me as well. They didn't know they were *different* from the animals they painted, they belonged.

My writing in the last chapters of *The Commune* is like that – every sentence flashes by like those gazelles – more than personal and not just impersonal. That's how I live, essentially – like a child: total openness – insecurity offset by buoyancy – enormous fears, enormous trust and dependence.